THE
FELTED BAG
BOOK

THE
FELTED BAG
BOOK

21 Simple Projects for Every Occasion

SUSIE JOHNS

St. Martin's Griffin
New York

www.stmartins.com

Library of Congress Cataloging-in-Publication Data Available Upon Request

ISBN: 978-0-312-61153-8

First published in 2009 by
New Holland Publishers (UK) Ltd

First U.S. Edition: January 2010

2 4 6 8 10 9 7 5 3 1

Senior Editor: Louise Coe
Photography: Paul Bricknell
Production: Marion Storz
Design: Lucy Parissi
Editorial Direction: Rosemary Wilkinson

Contents

Introduction

A handbag is not only a necessity, it is the finishing touch to your outfit. A good-looking bag is a great way to express your individuality and sense of style, not just a receptacle for all those necessary items such as money, keys, make-up and heaven knows what else.

Forget designer bags for the moment. Forget leather bags and bags made from canvas or plastic or snakeskin. Here is a selection of entirely different bags: those made from felt.

Felt is a great fabric. It's thick and strong — perfect for making beautiful, practical and hard-wearing bags. You can make felt in a number of ways: either by wet felting or needle felting with wool fibers, or by "boiling" woolen items.

This book introduces these various techniques to those unfamiliar with the felting genre, while also offering a number of new ideas and patterns for those who are already felting fans. The book is broken down into chapters on wet felting, knitting, crochet and recycling, offering fun and diverse projects to follow for each. It also encourages you to be imaginative and creative, with suggested variations on the main theme and plenty of scope for adaptation, using different colors and finishes. Each bag can be customized to express your individual sense of style. And once you have mastered the basic techniques, you can come up with your own ideas and create your own unique pieces.

Felt has a long history, probably dating back to the first time a pilgrim placed some sheep's wool inside his shoes to prevent blisters on a long journey, only to find that the heat, moisture and friction from his feet had compressed it into a piece of felt fabric.

Felt-making has been – and still is – practiced all over the world. In Scandinavia and Russia, the process is used to make boots and mittens; in Asia, large felt panels are used in the construction of yurts (a tent-like shelter used by nomads) and for capes worn by shepherds; in Turkey and other Middle Eastern countries you will find felt carpets and rugs; and in South America, the United States, the UK and numerous other countries it is it is used to make hats – and also in the manufacture of pianos and cars, among other practical applications. Felt-making is currently enjoying a big revival, with many artists, designers and craftsmen using the process in very creative ways to make clothing and household accessories.

Anyone who enjoys working with their hands, with fabrics and yarns in particular, can easily produce a simple felted bag. Start with combed wool fibers or with spun woolen yarn, if you prefer, and in no time at all, following the step-by-step projects in this book, you will be the proud owner of a delightful felt bag. So now is your chance to discover this craft for yourself and make a bag – or two or more – that is beautiful as well as practical and hard-wearing.

It is fascinating to witness the process of soft woolen fibers being transformed into thick felted fabric, and particularly satisfying, in the case of the knitted and crocheted bags, which are felted in a domestic washing machine, to know that you intended to shrink them to a fraction of their original size, and did not do it by accident, as many of us have done at some time with a beloved sweater or scarf.

I have enjoyed making the bags in this book and hope that you will be inspired to try some of the projects for yourself.

SUSIE JOHNS

Basic information

The materials and equipment needed to make a felted bag will vary according to the technique you have chosen to use – whether it is wet felting, knitting, crochet or recycling. If you turn to the beginning of each chapter, you will find a more detailed list of all the items you will require.

Many craft shops and yarn shops carry a range of specialist materials for felting, such as wool fleece, yarns, crochet hooks and needles, and some can be real treasure troves when it comes to other items such as buttons, bag handles and clasps. However there is no doubt that buying on the internet has made shopping a whole lot easier; you will find a whole range of useful materials and equipment by typing "felting" into a search engine, or by browsing online craft catalogs.

Hoarders among you may find a use for old wool and cashmere sweaters (even those that have been attacked by moths) and stashes of knitting yarn. Those who enjoy browsing in resale shops and flea markets should be on the lookout for pure wool garments that can be recycled, as well as second-hand knitting needles, crochet hooks, buttons and old handbags that can be dismantled or deconstructed, giving attractive handles, buckles or clasps a new lease of life.

Try techniques such as needle felting (top) on small swatches, and knit (or crochet) a small test piece (bottom) before tackling a larger project

Wool

The most important material is, of course, wool. This may come in the form of **wool tops**, which is wool fleece that has been carded (combed) so that all the fibers run in the same direction. It is sold in thick lengths, like a rope, and is used for wet felting and needle felting. The desired quantity can be gently teased away, or the whole rope, or part of it, can be rolled to make bag handles and straps.

Perhaps a more familiar way to purchase wool is in spun form, in **skeins**, **hanks** or **balls**. These can be used to make knitted or crocheted fabrics, which can then be felted by shrinking them in the washing machine.

Ready-made **woolen garments**, such as scarves, sweaters, shawls and woolen blankets, can also be turned into felt. This is a great way to recycle fabrics that may otherwise be consigned to landfill.

You can also buy **ready-made felt**, manufactured from wool or a wool-viscose mix, for quick and easy results. Do not confuse this with the squares of craft felt available in art shops and toy stores, which is not suitable for use in any of the projects in this book.

Lining

Most of the projects in this book do not require a lining. Knitted and crocheted felt, when shrunk in a washing machine, tends to produce a thick, firm fabric, and wet felt can be made to your preferred thickness, depending on how many layers of fibers you build up.

Recycled felt, meanwhile, where you shrink existing garments or other woolen items in hot water, can vary depending on the original thickness. If the resulting felted fabric is a little too soft or stretchy, a lining may help to give it substance and make it more hard-wearing.

As well as reinforcing your bag, a lining can also provide a soft, smooth interior, in contrast to the warm, woolly texture of the felt.

To line a bag, choose a plain or patterned **silk**, **cotton** or **synthetic fabric**. Measure the bag and cut the fabric to fit the front and back, as well as the base and sides for a deeper bag, adding 2 cm (¾ in) all round for seams and turnings. You should aim to make your fabric lining into a bag of the same dimensions as the bag to be lined. Next place the lining inside the bag, with wrong sides together, then turn under any raw edges and slipstitch the fold to the top of the bag. To make the lining as inconspicuous as possible, position it a little way down from the top edge of the bag.

AFTER-CARE: Remember to treat felted items as you would any woolen items. Dry cleaning is recommended. If you prefer washing, it is best to do this by hand; you may be able to wash them in your washing machine on a wool cycle. Washing may distort the shape and you will probably have to ease them back into shape while damp.

ABBREVIATIONS

beg	begin(ning)
cm	centimeter(s)
sc	single crochet
dec	decrease
in	inch(es)
inc	increase
k	knit
mm	millimeters
p	purl
psso	pass slipped stitch over
rep	repeat
sl 1	slip one stitch
st(s)	stitch(es)
tbl	through back of loop(s)
tog	together
*****	repeat instructions between asterisks as many times as instructed
( )	work instructions inside brackets as many times as instructed

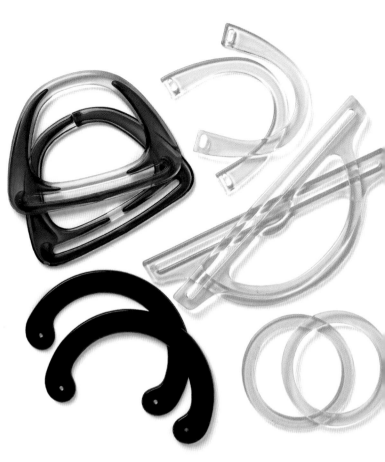

Look out for beautiful buttons for the perfect finishing touch. Sew on firmly with a needle and strong thread.

Rigid handles can give a professional finish. These are acrylic, but also look out for wood and bamboo.

To line handles and straps, you can use the same fabric or – better still – use a length of **ribbon** or **tape** the same width as, or slightly narrower than, the handle. **Velvet ribbon** is a good choice for this, as it creates a slip-proof handle that will sit comfortably on your shoulder (as with Mary, on page 44).

To further reinforce the bag, you may wish to create an **interlining**. This is probably best made from a non-woven interfacing, which is available in a range of different weights. For a really rigid result, choose **pelmet interfacing**, which is very firm and will hold its shape; it is particularly good for boxy-shaped bags. **Plastic canvas**, usually sold alongside tapestry canvasses, can also be employed, particularly for reinforcing bag bases – as with Eve, on page 59.

Fastenings

Buttons come in different shapes, sizes and materials and are the perfect choice for a simple fastening. Check out craft shops for other fastenings too, as it is easy to substitute one that really catches your eye for any of those used in the book.

Snap fasteners are useful for keeping bag flaps closed (see page 42 for an example of this). You may also wish to consider a **magnetic closure** for a more professional finish. These come in two main parts, with metal washers, and are easy to insert into the fabric, and to attach with the help of a hammer or pliers (see pages 54–55 for instructions on how to do this).

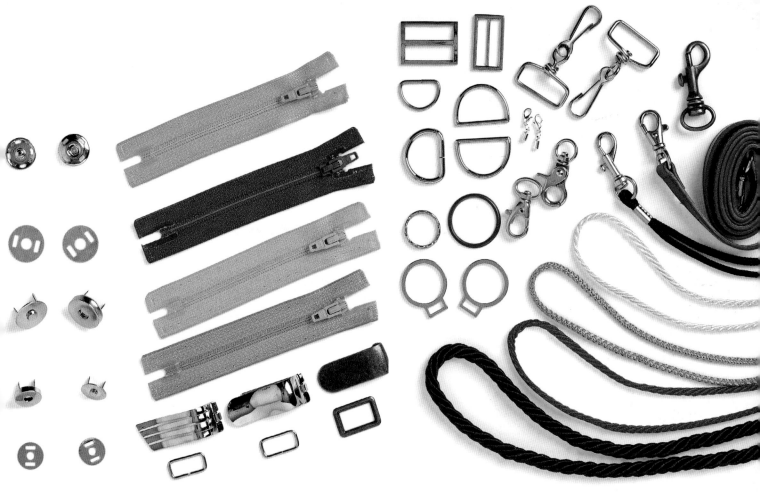

Experiment with fastenings and closures, such as snap fasteners, magnets, zippers, and hinged clasps.

Cord handles and straps can be stitched directly to a felt bag or attached using various rings and clips.

Handles

Most of the bags in the book have felt handles but in some cases handles made from other materials have been used. Look for **wooden, acrylic** and **bamboo handles**, as well as **chains** and **cords**.

Tools

Aside from the equipment listed in each chapter, make sure you have a good pair of sturdy **dressmaking scissors** for cutting felted fabric, a smaller pair of scissors for snipping threads, and another pair of scissors that can be used for cutting paper and other materials for templates and patterns.

A large, sharp **embroidery needle** is useful for stitching through one or more thickness of felt, especially with embroidery threads, while a **blunt-ended tapestry needle** with a large eye is essential for joining knitted or crocheted pieces prior to felting. An all-purpose **sewing needle** is also used throughout the book, with ordinary sewing thread.

You will need a **tape measure** for measuring pattern pieces and a **rigid ruler** for checking gauge swatches and drawing straight lines.

Pens and **pencils** are always useful; a **water-erasable** or **fading fabric marker** is a good choice for making temporary marks on fabric, while an ordinary pencil or ballpoint pen can also be used for marking fabric, as well as patterns and templates.

Some of the templates on pages 106–109 have been reduced in size to fit them on the page, so it would be useful to have access to a **photocopier**, to enlarge these.

Wet felting

This traditional method of wet felting produces a very strong, thick and durable fabric by laying carded (combed) fibers of pure wool fleece in layers and matting them together into a dense mat, with the help of water, soap, heat and friction.

Materials

The fibers used for "wet" felting are sold as "wool tops" or "roving" but are generally referred to in this book as "fleece".

The bags in this section of the book are made with 21-micron merino wool tops: clean, carded (combed) fibers made from 100 percent wool from merino sheep. Merino wool tops are the most widely available and commonly used, probably because they tend to be the easiest to work with. They come in a wide range of colors (see the picture of felted beads on page 19 for some of the colors available).

Buy wool tops in small amounts and try to use them quickly. Storing the fibers for long periods of time makes them more difficult to pull apart. They are also troublesome to store, as keeping them in sealed plastic bags, which may seem the best idea if you want to protect them from moth damage, has the negative effect of retaining moisture, which can make the fibers coarse.

Basic equipment

Plastic sheet: This is to protect your work surface. Buy plastic sheeting from a DIY store or use a large garbage bag.

Towels: An old towel laid on top of the plastic sheet helps to soak up water. It is also useful to have a few towels handy for drying your hands and mopping up excess water.

Bubble wrap: Laid underneath the wool fibers, the texture of the bubble wrap helps to increase friction while you are rubbing, thereby speeding up the felting process.

Netting: This is laid on top of the fibers so that you can rub without disturbing the layers. The holes in the fabric allow water and soap to pass through. Use an old net curtain, a

mosquito net or length of medium-weight nylon or polyester netting.

Plastic bottle: Recycle any suitable plastic bottle. You will need to make a few holes in the cap with a sharp needle, such as a felting needle, so you can sprinkle the water on the felt. You could also use a plant spray bottle or a water bottle with a sports cap.

Block of soap: Choose a large block of soap; this is used to rub over the layers of wool fibers. An olive oil soap is a good choice, as it is kinder to your hands.

Bamboo mat: This can be used underneath the felt, instead of bubble wrap. It is also used in the later stages, if the felt needs to be rolled. For large pieces, use an old bamboo blind; for smaller pieces, a place mat or sushi mat is ideal.

Plastic: This is useful for cutting templates to create the desired size and shape and to prevent the layers of wool

step 2

step 3

step 4

from bonding together when making a bag in one piece. If you use a fairly rigid plastic, you can feel the hard edges of the shape as you felt. However, a thick plastic shopping bag is adequate. Buy sheets of acetate from an art supplier or look out for suitable packaging that can be recycled.

Scissors: To cut felt it is best to use dressmaking scissors. Embroidery scissors, small with sharp points, are also useful.

Markers: Use an erasable fabric marker or tailor's chalk to mark fabric, and a ballpoint pen or permanent marker to draw templates on plastic.

Needles: You will need an ordinary sewing needle and thread to stitch handles to some of the bags and a beading needle and strong thread to sew on beads and other decorations.

Method

The technique of creating "wet" felt varies in small details but basically involves creating layers of carded fleece and, with the aid of soap, water and friction, causing the fibers to bond together. The first part of the felting process creates pre-felt. This means that the fibers are bonded but not yet completely felted. The pre-felt can be cut and used to decorate other pieces, or you can proceed with the second part of the process, to create the finished felted fabric.

Felting

1 Prepare your work surface by protecting it with a plastic sheet and laying a towel and a layer of bubble wrap on top.

2 Tease out tufts of wool fleece. To do this, hold a long length of merino wool tops in one hand and, with the other hand, grasp the ends of the fibers tightly and pull.

step 5

step 6

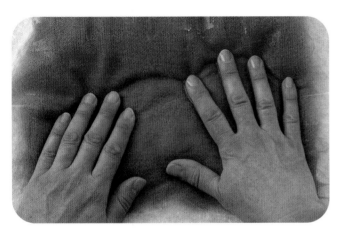

step 7

step 8

3 For the first layer, lay the fibers side by side on the work surface (or on the template, if you are using one), making sure that all the fibers lie in one direction and there is an even thickness all over. The felting process will cause the wool to shrink, so make sure you allow for this by adding about 15 to 20 percent more fabric all round than the desired measurement of the finished piece.

4 For the second layer, lay the fibers at right angles to the first layer, again making sure that the layer is of an even thickness.

5 For the third layer, the fibers should lie in the same direction as the first layer, and so on, until you have the desired number of layers.

6 To make the pre-felt, cover the layers of wool fibers with a piece of netting and, using the plastic bottle with holes pierced in the top, sprinkle with water, making sure the piece is evenly wetted but not soaking.

7 Pat it all over with your hands; this helps to settle the fibers, allowing a greater degree of control before the felting.

8 Gently rub the block of soap over the netting. This will start to felt the wool fibers. Do this as gently as possible in the early stages in order not to disturb the layers too much.

9 Press down all over with your hands, to make sure any air bubbles are removed before starting the felting.

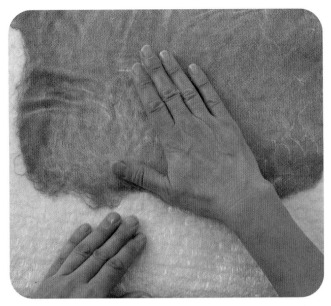

step 10

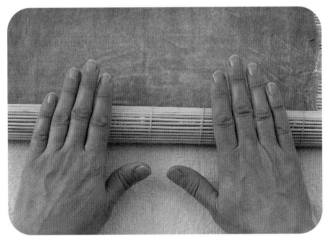

step 12

step 13

10 Rub with both hands, using a circular motion, for about 10 minutes.

11 Peel off the netting, turn the piece over, place the netting on top again and repeat the process on the other side. From time to time, lift the netting and replace it, to make sure it does not become embedded in the felted fibers.

12 To complete the felting process, place the pre-felt on a bamboo mat and roll it backwards and forwards for about 10 to 15 minutes, until the felt hardens, periodically wetting it with soapy water. Check the size from time to time and roll as required in different directions until you have achieved the desired shape and size.

13 Rinse the felt with really hot water. Place the felt in a bowl or sink and carefully pour boiling water (from a kettle) over. Repeat several times, then rinse under a cold running tap to remove soap residue.

14 Pull the felt gently into shape then lay out flat and allow to dry.

How to make felt beads

These can be used as fastenings or embellishments and are a good way of using up small amounts of leftover wool tops.

1 Twirl a small piece of fleece around your fingertip, then begin to wrap more fibers around it, to make a ball.

2 Wet the ball by dipping it briefly into a bowl of water or spraying it with water; squeeze out any excess water as it should be wet right through but not dripping.

3 Rub your hands with soap, then roll the ball gently in your palms, without using too much pressure. Continue until the ball begins to harden – about 10 minutes.

4 Roll the ball on a bamboo mat until it becomes very firm.

5 Place the ball in a sink or bowl and pour on very hot water from a kettle. Rinse thoroughly with cold water to remove soap.

How to make a felt cord

Felt cord makes useful handles; short lengths can be used to make button loops and decorations.

1 Pull off a length of fleece about 15–20 percent longer than the required finished length of the cord. Lay it on a work surface and sprinkle with water.

2 Wet your hands and soap them thoroughly, then draw the fibers through your hands, rolling them backwards and forwards. Keep rolling and wetting the fibers until they thicken.

3 Roll well on a bamboo mat or bubble wrap until the piece has hardened.

4 Once the cord is the required length and thickness, place in a bowl or sink and pour on really hot water from a kettle, then rinse with cold water and leave to dry.

step 2

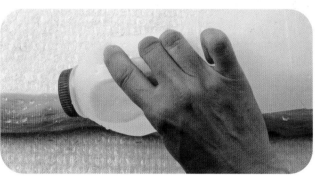

step 1

step 3

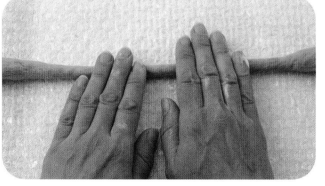

step 2

Scarlett

Made in one piece, this little handbag is quick and easy to make. You can make your bag bigger or smaller by altering the size of the template. Leave it plain or embellish it with felt beads – it's up to you.

Materials:

180 g (6⅓ oz) merino wool tops in red

180 g (6⅓ oz) merino wool tops in pink

Equipment

plastic sheet

old towel

bubble wrap

piece of plastic, approx. 30 x 30 cm (12 x 12 in)

netting

plastic bottle of water

soap

Finished size

width: 22 cm (8¾ in)

height: 26 cm (10¼ in)

Method

1 Place a sheet of plastic and a towel on your work surface with a sheet of bubble wrap on top. Cut a template from plastic to the size and shape of the finished bag, using the template on page 106 as a guide.

2 Split the red and pink wool fibers into two equal batches, for the front and back of the bag.

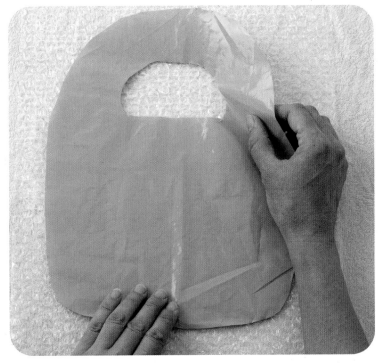

step 1

step 3

step 4

step 9

3 Lay three layers of the red and pink fibers onto the template.

4 Cover with the netting and sprinkle with water; ensure the piece is wet all over, but not soaking.

5 Gently rub the block of soap all over the netting. Press down to make sure all the air bubbles are removed before starting the felting process.

6 Rub with both hands, using a circular motion, for about 10 minutes. Turn the shape over and repeat the process on the other side. From time to time, lift the netting and replace it, to make sure it does not become embedded in the felted fibers.

7 Lay out three further layers of the red and pink fibers on the pre-felt and repeat the felting process. Turn the piece occasionally and make sure you fold the edges around the template to the back.

8 Now turn the whole piece over and cover the second side with three layers of pink and red fibers. Felt the second side and turn in the edges of the fibers to create a smooth and even edge around the template. Repeat with three more layers.

9 Once the felt has shrunk to the desired size and all fibers are nicely felted together, remove the template. To do this, cut the bag above the handles.

10 Trim the edges of the bag with scissors, if necessary, to correct the shape, then felt the cut edges by rubbing them with soapy fingers.

11 Now wet the bag with really hot water, and continue to felt, if necessary. Then place the felted bag in a sink or bowl and rinse with really hot water from a kettle. Rinse thoroughly with cold water to remove the soap, then gently pull the bag into shape and allow to dry flat.

Alina

This patchwork shoulder bag is made from a four-layered piece of flat felt. The random patches of color add charm to the design and can be varied, offering plenty of scope for individual expression.

Materials

200 g (7 oz) merino wool tops in red
80 g (2¾ oz) merino wool tops in purple
80 g (2¾ oz) merino wool tops in pale pink
80 g (2¾ oz) merino wool tops in hot pink
80 g (2¾ oz) merino wool tops in yellow
matching red sewing thread
embroidery thread in lilac
red felt bead

Equipment

plastic sheet
old towel
bubble wrap
netting
plastic bottle of water
soap
bamboo mat
embroidery needle

Finished size

width: 34 cm (13½ in)
height: 28 cm (11 in)

Method

1 Protect your work surface with a plastic sheet. Place an old towel on top and a sheet of bubble wrap on top of the towel.

2 Reserve about a quarter of the red merino wool tops for the handle and lay out the remainder in four layers to form a large rectangle about 110 x 60 cm (43$\frac{1}{3}$ x 23$\frac{2}{3}$ in). After felting, you should have a finished piece measuring about 100 x 50 cm (39$\frac{1}{3}$ x 19$\frac{2}{3}$ in).

3 Lay the netting over the top and sprinkle with water, making sure the wool fibers are evenly wetted but not soaking wet.

4 Gently rub the block of soap all over the netting. Press down all over with your hands to make sure any air bubbles are removed before starting the felting process.

5 Rub with both hands, using a circular motion, for about 10 minutes, to create the pre-felt. From time to time, lift the netting and replace it to make sure it does not become embedded in the felted fibers. Turn the whole piece over from time to time, to achieve the same felted effect on both sides.

6 To create the patchwork design, remove the netting and place patches of purple, pale pink, hot pink and yellow fibers on the pre-felt, using the picture of the finished bag as a guide.

7 Replace the netting and sprinkle with water, then gently rub all over with the block of soap.

8 Rub for about 15 minutes or until the wool tops are well bonded to the backing.

9 Turn the piece over from time to time, to achieve the same felted effect on both sides.

step 6

step 7

step 8

10 When the fibers are well bonded, place the piece on a bamboo mat and roll well for about 10 minutes or until the piece has hardened.

11 Once the fibers are firmly bonded together, wet the piece with really hot water and continue rolling if necessary. As soon as you start using hot water, the felt will shrink a little more.

12 Place the felted piece in a sink or bowl and pour on really hot water from a kettle. Pull the piece into shape with your hands, lay it on a flat surface and allow to dry while you felt the handles and cut out the templates.

Handle

13 To make the handle, which also forms the sides of the bag, you will need to end up with a piece measuring 110 x 5 cm (43$\frac{1}{3}$ in x 2 in). Lay down a long strip of red fibers on the prepared work surface, measuring about 160 cm (63 in) long and 8 cm (3$\frac{1}{4}$ in) wide. Cover with the netting, sprinkle with water and gently rub with the block of soap.

14 Continue with the felting process, as described for the main part of the bag, to produce a thick, strong strap.

Making up

15 Cut out three pieces from the patchworked felt: one piece measuring 50 x 35 cm (19$\frac{2}{3}$ x 13$\frac{3}{4}$ in) for the back and flap, one piece measuring 35 x 25 cm (13$\frac{3}{4}$ x 10 in) for the front and one piece measuring 25 x 4 cm (10 x 1$\frac{1}{2}$) for the base.

16 Stitch the bag front to the base using an embroidery needle and lilac embroidery thread and using blanket stitch to create raised seams about 0.5 cm ($\frac{1}{4}$ in) from the edge of the felt. Stitch the back to the base the same way. Stitch the strap in place, with the ends forming the side pieces of the bag. Decorate the edge of the flap and the strap with blanket stitch.

17 As a final embellishment, cut an 8 cm (3$\frac{1}{4}$ in) circle of pink felt from leftover pieces and a 4 cm (1$\frac{1}{2}$ in) circle of purple felt. Snip into the edges to form fringed "petals". Stitch to the bag through the center of each circle, adding a red felt bead in the circle.

NOTE: Remember to save any scraps of felt – trimmings cut from larger pieces, or small experimental swatches – as they can be used to add decorative touches, such as this disc-shaped flower.

Annie

With a cord handle long enough to fit over your shoulder or across your body, this is the ideal all-purpose bag. You can make it in the color shown or a color to suit every outfit.

Materials

180 g (6⅓ oz) merino wool tops in dark purple

180 g (6⅓ oz) merino wool tops in thistle lilac

matching lilac sewing thread

Equipment

plastic sheet

old towel

bubble wrap

piece of plastic, at least 29 x 25 cm (11½ x 10 in)

netting

plastic bottle of water

soap

sewing needle

4 dark purple felt beads

40 cm (16 in) lilac silky cord

Finished size

height: 24 cm (9½ in)

width: 24 cm (9½ in)

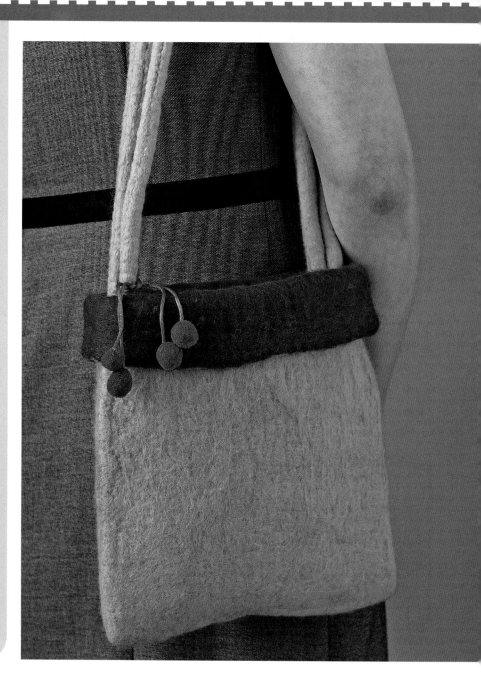

Method

1. Protect your work surface with the plastic sheet, then lay the towel and bubble wrap on top.

2. Cut a template measuring 29 x 25 cm (11½ x 10 in), from the piece of plastic and place on the bubble wrap.

3. Reserve 40 g (1½ oz) of the lilac wool tops for the handle. Divide the remaining lilac fibers into two equal batches, to make the front and back of the bag, and set aside.

4. Place the template on the work surface and lay three layers of dark purple fibers on top. Add at least 5 cm (2 in) extra all round the edge of template for shrinkage.

5. Cover with the netting and sprinkle with water, making sure the piece is evenly wetted but not soaked. Gently rub the block of soap over the netting.

6. Press down all over to make sure any air bubbles are removed before starting the felting process, then rub with both hands, using a circular motion, for about 10 minutes. From time to time, lift the netting and replace it, to make sure that it does not become embedded in the felted fibers.

7. Turn the piece over with the felted side face down and the template face up. Bring the edges of the felt around the edges of the template.

8. Lay out three layers of dark purple on the template, cover with the netting and pre-felt it in the same way as the first side.

9. Wrap the edges of the fibers around the template and continue felting to fuse the edges of the front and back of the bag together. Take care that you do not felt it too much at this stage, however, or the next layer will not adhere.

10. Cover the bag, first one side and then the other, with three layers of thistle lilac fibers and pre-felt them. The lilac layers should completely cover the layers of dark purple.

step 4

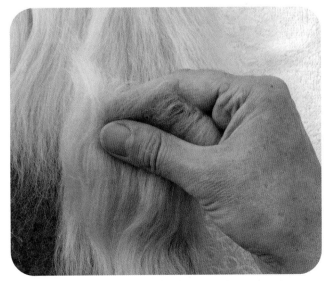

step 10

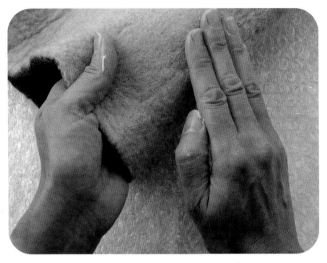

step 11

step 13

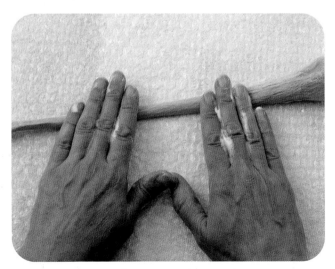

step 14

11 Cut the bag open at the top end. Felt the ends into the bag and proceed to finish felting the whole bag. Rub the cut edges and the joined areas at the sides and base of the bag with soapy fingers.

12 Once the felt has shrunk to the desired size and all the fibers are nicely felted together, remove the template. Place the bag in a sink or bowl and rinse with really hot water from a kettle. Rinse again several times with really hot water. Roll down the top edge and pull the bag gently into shape, then allow to dry flat.

Handles

13 To make the handles, use the reserved fibers to make three cords. Lay three 110 cm (43⅓ in) strands of wool tops on the work surface. Sprinkle each one with water, then wet your hands and soap them thoroughly.

14 Roll the wool cords backwards and forwards. Keep rolling and wetting them until they thicken and form neat cords. Each one will shrink in length to about 90 cm (35½ in). Once it is the required length and thickness, leave to dry.

Finishing

15 Stitch the three handle cords together neatly and firmly, side by side, using lilac sewing thread. Stitch the ends of the cords to the inside of the bag.

16 Cut the lilac silky cord in half and stitch a felt bead to each of the four ends. Tie to the base of the handle.

Harriet

This simple stylish bag is the ideal size for carrying the everyday bare necessities such as a purse, mobile phone and make-up. If you like, you can make the strap longer to wear across the body or you could leave it off altogether to make a stylish clutch.

Materials

200 g (7 oz) merino wool tops in blue

100 g (3½ oz) merino wool tops in turquoise

100 g (3½ oz) merino wool tops in light blue

matching blue sewing thread

clasp or buckle

Equipment

plastic sheet

old towel

bubble wrap

piece of plastic, at least 30 x 28 cm (12 x 11 in)

netting

plastic bottle of water

soap

sewing needle

Finished size

height: 15 cm (6 in)

width: 28 cm (11 in)

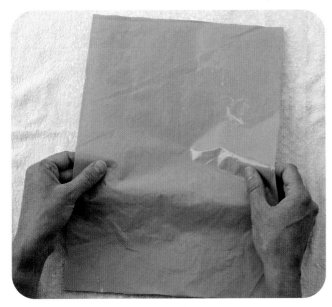

step 2

step 4

1 Protect your work surface with the plastic sheet and lay the towel and bubble wrap on top.

2 Cut a template measuring 30 x 28 cm (12 x 11 in), from plastic, and place it on the bubble wrap.

3 Lay out three layers of the blue fibers on top of the template, adding at least 5 cm (2 in) extra all round for shrinkage.

4 In the middle of the piece lay out another three layers of blue. On the top of the piece and the top half of the sides, lay out three layers of turquoise and blue. On the bottom and bottom half of the sides, lay out three layers of dark blue. The positioning of the colors is important: if you wish to create a striped effect, lay out the fibers in blocks of separate colors; if you want a more random effect, lay the fibers in smaller, irregular patches. Make sure the different colored areas are all the same thickness, creating an even layer of fibers overall.

5 Lay the netting over the top and sprinkle with water, making sure the wool fibers are evenly wetted but not too wet. Gently rub the block of soap over the netting. Press down all over with your hands to remove any air bubbles before starting the felting process.

6 Rub with both hands, using a circular motion, for about 10 minutes. Occasionally lift the netting and replace it to ensure it does not become embedded in the felted fibers.

7 Turn the felt and template over. Fold the edges of the pre-felted piece over the edges of the template.

step 8

step 12

8 Cover the bottom half of the template with three layers of blue and dark blue. This will form the front of the bag; the felt behind the template will form the back and flap.

9 Repeat the felting process for this part of the bag. Turn the piece from time to time and felt all edges and ends into the bag using soapy fingers.

10 Continue to work on the bag until the felt is nice and strong. Once the felt has shrunk to the desired size and all the fibers are nicely felted together, remove the template.

11 Now rinse the felted bag with really hot water. To do this, place the bag in a bowl or sink and pour really hot water from a kettle over it. Rinse several times with hot then cold water, then pull the bag gently into shape and allow to dry flat.

Handle

12 To make the strap, lay at least two layers of dark blue wool tops in a row 150 cm (59 in) long on a piece of bubble wrap. Wet the fibers, place the netting on top and pre-felt. If the netting is shorter than the length of fibers, work on one area at a time, ensuring each area is pre-felted before lifting the netting and moving on to another area.

13 Use soapy fingers to felt the strap edges, making them smooth and even. If necessary, trim the edges with scissors to obtain a neat line, then work over the cut edges with soapy fingers. Rinse the strap and leave to dry.

Finishing

14 When the felted pieces are completely dry, stitch the handle ends to the inside of the bag.

15 Stitch one half of the clasp or buckle to the front of the bag and the other to the flap. In the finished picture a two-part ceramic buckle with a magnetic closure has been used.

Emma

This bucket-shaped bag is constructed from a large piece of flat felt with two rolled felt handles and a pretty appliqué design on the front.

Materials

300 g (10 oz) merino wool tops in natural white

80 g (2³/₄ oz) merino wool tops in light yellow

80 g (2³/₄ oz) merino wool tops in light pink

80 g (2³/₄ oz) merino wool tops in light turquoise

white or natural thread

embroidery threads in yellow, pink and turquoise

Equipment

plastic sheet

old towel

bubble wrap

netting

soap

plastic bottle of water

bamboo blind

pen, pencil or tailor's chalk

large crewel needle

embroidery needle

tissue paper

Finished size

height: 32 cm (12¹/₂ in)

width: 28 cm (11 in)

Method

1 Protect your work surface with a plastic sheet and place a towel and a sheet of bubble wrap on top.

2 Make a six-layered piece of flat felt by laying out the natural white fleece in six layers over an area measuring about 85 x 60 cm (33¹/₂ x 23²/₃ in). This allows for 5cm (2 in) shrinkage and should give you a piece measuring 75 x 50 cm (29¹/₂ x 19²/₃ in) after felting.

3 Cover with netting and sprinkle with water, making sure that the piece is evenly wetted but not soaking.

4 Gently rub the block of soap over the netting. Press down all over with your hands, to make sure any air bubbles are removed before starting the felting.

5 Once the wool has started bonding together, put a bamboo blind underneath and roll the felt from both sides, lengthwise and diagonally. The direction in which you roll is the direction in which the felt will shrink. If the felt piece is too big to roll on the bamboo, either roll it in sections or rub it with your hands.

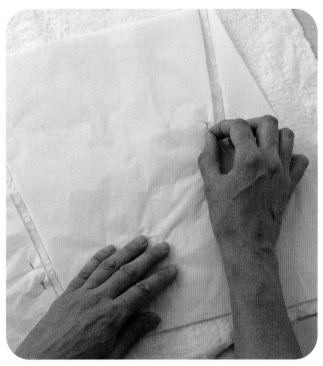

step 10

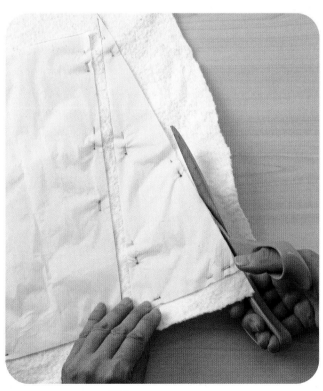

step 11

6 Once the felt has shrunk to the desired size and all the fibers are nicely felted together, place the felt in a bowl or sink and rinse with really hot water from a kettle. As soon as you start using hot water the felt will shrink a little more. Rinse thoroughly and gently squeeze out the excess water, then lay the felt out flat and leave to dry.

7 Make small squares, measuring about 15 cm (6 in), of yellow, pink and turquoise felt for the flower motifs in a similar way, but using only two layers of wool fibers instead of six.

Handle

8 To make a cord, lay a 70 cm (27½ in) length of wool tops on the work surface. Sprinkle with water, then wet your hands and soap them thoroughly, Roll the wool backwards and forwards to form a long sausage.

9 Keep rolling and wetting the felt until it thickens and forms a neat cord. It will shrink to about 60 cm (23⅔ in) in length. Once it is the required length and thickness, leave it to dry then cut it in half.

Making up

10 Cut out two templates from tissue paper for the front and back of the bag and two templates for the sides, using the patterns on page 107 as a guide. Cut out one rectangle measuring 19 x 4 cm (7½ x 1½ in) for the base.

11 Lay the templates on the felt, mark around the edges with a pen or tailor's chalk and cut out the felt pieces for the bag.

12 Cut the small colored felt pieces into petal and stem shapes (using the template on page 107 or creating your own design) and arrange them on the bag front (and the back, if you wish).

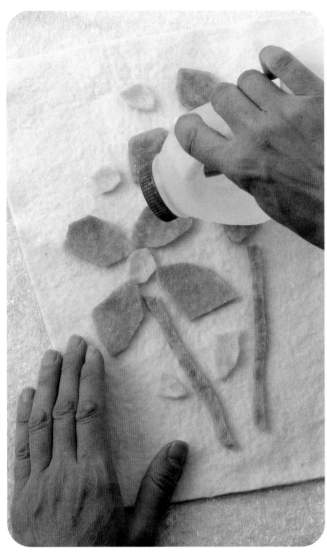

step 13

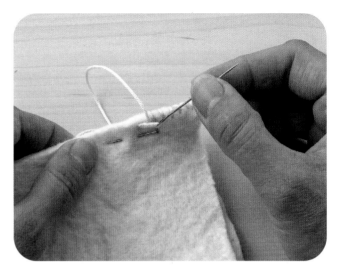

step 14

Finishing

13 Sprinkle the motifs with water and gently rub them with soapy fingers to attach them to the backing fabric. Rinse well to remove all soap residue. Leave to dry. Overstitch the edges of each shape, if you wish, with matching embroidery thread.

14 Using a sewing needle and white or natural thread, stitch the bag front to the sides, oversewing the edges to create raised seams. Stitch the bag back to the sides in the same way, and then stitch the base in place. Finally, pin and then stitch the handles in place.

NOTE: If you prefer, the colored patches for the flower motif can be needle felted (see page 98) onto the bag or simply stitched in place, rather than wet felting them. You could also recycle pieces left over from other projects if you don't wish to make small felt pieces especially for the decoration.

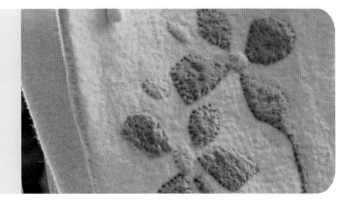

Knitting

Knitting is a relatively quick, easy and fuss-free way to create felted bags. The bags are made much bigger than you might imagine, as the felting process causes dramatic shrinkage in order to produce something that is firm and hard wearing.

Most of the projects in this book are knitted in garter stitch (knit every row). This not only makes them easy for even a novice knitter, it also creates a thick, solid fabric, perfect for a strong handbag. In fact, most of the finished bags are firm and dense enough not to require lining.

Garter stitch also creates a flat fabric that does not curl up, which is an advantage when felting in the washing machine. If edges curl, they may become bound in that curled-up position and, once this has happened, it is difficult to separate the fibers. This curling tendency can be exploited when it comes to making felted flower petals, however. Petals knitted in stockinette stitch have a natural tendency to curl and they can be left like this while drying; when completely dry they will retain their curled shape.

Yarns

All the yarns used in these projects are 100 percent wool. Occasionally, yarns made from wool mixed with a small proportion of other fibers will felt successfully but as a general rule of thumb it is best to stick to 100 percent wool. It is important to look carefully at the label, however, as yarns marked "machine washable" or "superwash", even if they are spun from 100 percent wool, will not felt.

Needles

Projects are usually knitted on needles larger than those recommended on the ball band of each individual yarn. Using bigger needles means that you use more yarn but this is necessary for good results. When the felting process takes place, the knitted fabric shrinks and thickens.

Gauge

In each project a gauge is given. This is a guideline so you can check to see if the gauge of your knitting matches the gauge stated. If you have *more* stitches to 10 cm (4 in) than stated, then try using needles one size larger; if you

Garter stitch

have fewer stitches, try using smaller needles. This information is also useful if you decide to substitute a different yarn from the one specified, as you will want one that knits to a similar gauge. Do be aware that if you use a different yarn your bag may end up bigger, smaller, wider or narrower than the one shown, and might even be a different texture.

Method

Knitting

When making up the knitted items, secure and trim off any loose ends. Normally loose ends are woven into the fabric, usually on the seams, but if the item is to be felted this is not only unnecessary but can cause lumps, bumps and uneven results.

Felting

Place the knitted items to be felted in a washing machine with two or three old small towels or face cloths. Do not use new towels as they are liable to shed fibers, which will become incorporated in the felt. Small towels are better than big ones

as a knitted item may get tangled in a large towel and become misshapen.

Add normal laundry detergent but no fabric softener. The items in this book were felted using an eco-friendly non-biological liquid detergent. Set the machine to a 40°C (100°F) cycle with the shortest possible spin. If you have a top-loading or twin-tub machine, you will be able to check on the progress of the felting at various stages but with a front-loading machine, you will have to wait until the end of the cycle.

During the wash cycle, the hot water causes the fibers to swell, while the agitation causes the scales on the fibers to rub together and form a bond. The knitting

A sample of knitting and the felted result

shrinks and forms a dense mat, not only smaller but also thicker and firmer than the original knitted fabric.

Once you have removed the felted items from the machine, check to see if they have felted successfully. If the texture of the stitches is still very apparent or if the fabric is too soft and loose, you may need to return the item to the machine and wash again at a higher temperature of 60°C (140°F). If you are happy with the texture, however, pull the items gently into shape while still damp and lay them out flat to dry.

Bear in mind that this is a somewhat experimental process and sometimes produces unexpected results. For example, if you place too many items in your machine, some of them may become joined together. Most of the time, however, the results are successful.

Drying

Do not tumble dry the items, as they may become misshapen or shrink even further and become hard. Do not hang them up to dry, as the water still contained in the fibers can be heavy and may cause the item to stretch out of shape.

Bear in mind that the drying process can take a long time. You may have to wait several days or even weeks, depending on temperature and humidity, for your felted fabric to dry completely.

When it is totally dry, if the fabric is suitably firm and dense, you will be able to cut it without the cut edges fraying. This means that the edges of bags do not need to be hemmed and that shapes and motifs can be cut from the felted fabric.

> **NOTE**: In some of the projects, the instructions refer to "right" and "wrong" sides of the material, but with garter stitch both sides of the fabric look the same, so do not worry which is the right or wrong side. Just make sure that you match row ends and sew cast-on or cast-off edges stitch by stitch to avoid puckering or distortion.

Valerie

This soft little shoulder bag features a silver chain strap and a sparkly brooch on its tab fastening, adding a touch of glamour – perfect for an evening out. It is very quick to make and requires only two balls of yarn.

Materials

2 x 50 g (1¾ oz) balls Rowan Kid Classic (153 yards) in lavender ice 841

matching purple sewing thread

2 x 2 cm (¾ in) rings

70 cm (27½ in) handbag chain with clips

1 large snap fastener

1 large decorative brooch or button

Equipment

pair of 6.50 mm (US: 10½) knitting needles

tapestry needle

sewing needle

Gauge

14 sts and 24 rows to 10 cm (4 in) measured over garter stitch using 6.50 mm (US: 10½) knitting needles

Finished size (approx.)

width: 24 cm (9½ in)

height: 16 cm (6¼ in)

Method

Front and back (make 2)

1 Cast on 60 sts and work 18 rows in garter stitch (knit every row).

2 Decrease 1 st at each end of next row and every following sixth row until 40 sts remain. Cast off loosely.

3 To make a tab, pick up and knit the center 10 sts of cast-off edge on one of the pieces and knit 28 rows. Cast off.

Making up

4 Stitch front to back along base and sides using the tapestry needle and spare yarn.

Felting

5 Place the bag in a washing machine with detergent but no fabric softener and wash at 40°C (100°F) with no spin (or minimum spin). Pull the bag gently into shape while wet, place on a flat surface and leave to dry naturally.

step 6

step 7

step 8

Finishing

6 Stitch rings in place at either side of the bag at the top of each side seam and attach the chain to the rings.

7 Stitch one half of the snap fastener on the underside of the tab and the other on the front of the bag.

8 Pin a brooch or stitch a button to the front of the tab.

Joan

Smaller bag

This version is 21 cm (8¼ in) wide and 11 cm (4¼ in) high and uses only one ball of yarn. For front and back (make 2), cast on 50 sts and work 12 rows in garter stitch (knit every row). Dec 1 st at each end of next and every following sixth row until 36 sts remain. Cast off. Make the tab and finish the bag, as larger version.

For a different type of fastening, attach a D-ring to the end of the tab and a hinged clip to the front of the bag. For a different handle, thread beads onto strong thread and stitch the ends to the bag.

Mary

This unusual asymmetrical shoulder bag combines two harmonious colors of yarn. To prevent the handle stretching too much in use, it is a good idea to line it with a length of velvet ribbon. If you wish, you could also line the main body of the bag.

Materials

5 x 25 g (1 oz) balls Jamieson & Smith 2-ply jumper-weight yarn (125 yards) in pale turquoise 75

6 x 25 g (1 oz) balls Jamieson & Smith 2-ply jumper-weight yarn (125 yards) in powder blue FC15

1.1 m (1¼ yd) of 38 mm (1½ in) wide velvet ribbon (optional)

sewing thread to match ribbon (optional)

2 silver flat rectangular rings, approx. 4 x 2 cm (1½ x ¾ in)

Equipment

pair of 7.00 mm (US: 10½) knitting needles

tapestry needle

sewing needle

Gauge

13 sts and 28 rows to 10 cm (4 in) measured over garter stitch using 7.00 mm (US: 10½) knitting needles and double yarn

Finished size (approx.)

width: 30 cm (12 in)

height 21 cm (8¼ in)

Method

Note that yarn is used double throughout.

Front

1 Cast on 50 sts in pale turquoise yarn and work in garter stitch (knit every row) for 64 rows.

2 To shape the strap extension, cast off 22 sts at beginning of next row (right side), then knit to end.
Next row and each wrong-side row: k to end.
Next 3 right-side rows: Cast off 3 sts, k to end.
Next 3 right-side rows: Cast off 2 sts, k to end.
Next 3 right-side rows: Cast off 1 st, k to end.
Cast off remaining 10 sts.

Back

3 Follow the instructions for the front, working in the powder blue yarn.

Shoulder strap

4 Cast on 10 sts in powder blue yarn and work in garter stitch for 226 rows or until the work measures 104 cm (41 in). Cast off.

step 9

step 10

step 11

Pocket

5 Cast on 23 sts in powder blue yarn and work 25 rows in garter stitch. Cast off.

Making up

6 Stitch pocket to center front, using tapestry needle and yarn. Stitch front to back along base and sides.

Felting

7 Place the bag and the shoulder strap in a washing machine and wash at 40°C (100°F) with a normal powder or liquid detergent; do not use fabric softener and do not spin.

8 Remove from the machine, squeeze out excess water, pull gently into shape and leave to dry flat; do not hang up.

Finishing

9 Stitch the velvet ribbon, if using, to one side of the shoulder strap, using matching sewing thread.

10 Insert one end of the shoulder strap into a metal ring, then fold over and stitch neatly.

11 Insert the strap extension on the front of the bag into the other side of the metal ring, fold over and stitch. Repeat on the back of the bag.

Fred

Matching slipcase

You can use any leftover yarn to make a matching slipcase, useful for protecting a camera, MP3 player or other device, or for separating your passport or other important documents from the other clutter inside your bag. To make a slipcase like the one below, which measures 16 cm (6 ¼ in) high and 15 cm (6 in) wide, cast on 23 sts and work 100 rows in garter stitch. Cast off. Fold in half and stitch the side seams using matching yarn. To felt, follow the instructions for the main bag. Cut a 32 cm (12 ½ in) length of ribbon and stitch in place around the top of the slipcase, about 6 mm (¼ in) from the edge.

Juliet

This slouchy bag has a spacious interior – perfect for a trip to the shops or the beach.
It is shown here in two different color schemes: purple and turquoise, and blue and pink.
Instructions are given for the purple/turquoise bag, with the blue/pink option in brackets.

Materials

1 x 100 g (3½ oz) ball Knitshop Simply Wool
(219 yards) in blue-turquoise (or blue)

1 x 100 g (3½ oz) ball Knitshop Simply Wool
(219 yards) in dark lilac (or bright lilac)

1 x 100 g (3½ oz) ball Knitshop Simply Wool
(219 yards) in bright lilac (or rose pink)

1 x 100 g (3½ oz) ball Knitshop Simply Wool
(219 yards) in light lilac (or deep pink)

Equipment

pair of 7.00 mm (US: 10½) knitting needles

tapestry needle

cookie tin or similar rectangular object

Gauge

13 stitches and 23 rows to 10 cm (4 in)
measured over garter stitch using 7.00 mm
(US: 10½) knitting needles

Finished size (approx.)

width: 22 cm (8¾ in)

height: 20 cm (8 in)

Method

Sides (make 2)

1 Cast on 70 sts in blue-turquoise (or blue) and work 36 rows in garter stitch.

2 Break yarn, join in dark lilac (or bright lilac) and work 36 rows in garter stitch.

3 Break yarn, join in bright lilac (or rose pink) and work 36 rows in garter stitch.

4 Break yarn, join in light lilac (deep pink) and work 4 rows.

5 Cast off 18 sts at beg of next 2 rows and 1 st at beg of next 8 rows. Work 2 rows without decreases, then dec 1 st at beg of next 2 rows. For the handle, work 120 rows on remaining 24 sts. Cast off.

step 6

Making up

6 Join the two side pieces together using matching yarn, then flatten the bag so that the seams are at the center front and back of the bag.

7 Stitch the base seam and stitch the two handle ends together.

Felting

8 Place the bag in a washing machine and wash at 40°C (100°F) with a normal powder or liquid detergent; do not use fabric softener and do not spin.

9 Remove from the machine, squeeze out excess water and pull gently into shape. Insert a cookie tin or a similar object of a suitable size and shape to help create a rectangular shape. Leave to dry completely before removing the tin.

step 9

Juniper

Shallower bag

This version has a slightly shorter handle and makes a good shoulder bag big enough to accommodate a magazine or folder. It is made from a shaded yarn in fruity colors.

You will need two 50 g (1¾ oz) balls of Wendy Fusion (96 yards) in shade 155 cajun and two balls in shade 158 juniper berries.

With 7.00 mm (US: 10½) needles and shade 155, working to a gauge of 13 stitches and 25 rows to 10 cm (4 in), cast on 70 sts and work 72 rows of garter stitch, joining in shade 158 when the first ball has run out.

Cast off 18 sts at beg of next 2 rows, 1 st at beg of next 8 rows, work 2 rows without decreases, then dec 1 st at beg of next 2 rows.

Continue on these 24 remaining sts until the yarn runs out.

Make the other half of the bag in exactly the same way and make up and felt as for the main bag.

Violet

Quick and easy to knit, this little clutch purse takes only one ball of yarn. The felted fabric is firm, so lining is optional. You can use scraps of left-over felted fabric from another project to make the decoration, or you can buy ready-made wool-viscose felt.

Materials

1 x 100 g (3½ oz) ball Rowan Scottish Tweed Aran (186 yards) in lavender 005

magnetic closure

10 cm (4 in) square of orange felt

8 cm (3¼ in) square of pink felt

matching lavender sewing thread

lining fabric, at least 35 x 50 cm (13¾ x 19⅔ in)

large decorative button

Equipment

pair of 5.50 mm (US: 9) knitting needles

tapestry needle

sewing needle

flat-nosed pliers

pen, pencil or tailor's chalk

Gauge

13 sts and 28 rows to 10 cm (4 in) measured over garter stitch using 5.50 mm (US: 9) knitting needles

Finished size (approx.)

width: 28 cm (11 in)

height: 15 cm (6 in)

Method

1 Cast on 40 sts in lavender yarn and work 80 rows in garter stitch (knit every row).

2 To shape the flap, dec 1 st at beginning of each row until 18 sts remain, then dec 2 sts at beginning of next 6 rows. Cast off remaining 6 sts.

Making up

3 Fold the main part of the bag (excluding flap) in half, with right sides together, so the fold reaches just under the tab of the bag and stitch side seams using the tapestry needle and spare yarn. Turn right side out.

Felting

4 Place the bag in a washing machine and wash at 40°C (100°F) with a normal powder or liquid detergent; do not use fabric softener and do not spin.

5 Remove from the machine, squeeze out excess water, pull gently into shape and leave to dry flat; do not hang up.

step 6

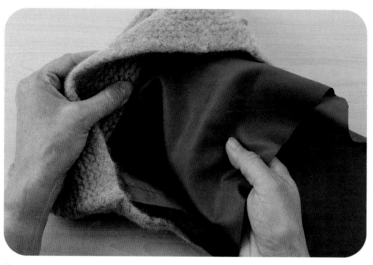

step 7

step 8

Finishing

6 Insert one half of the magnetic closure into the front of the bag, to correspond with the lower part of the flap.

7 Place the bag on the lining fabric and use it as a guide to cut out the lining. Stitch the side seams of the lining and place inside the bag.

8 Fold under raw edges and slipstitch in place.

9 Fix the other half of the magnetic closure to the underside of the flap; on the front of the flap, bend over the prongs using pliers, making sure they are pressed down flat and as firmly as possible.

10 Mark a 9 cm (3 ½ in) circle on the orange felt square and a 7 cm (2 ¾ in) circle on the pink felt square; to do this, draw around suitable round objects, such as cups or lids. Cut out the circles.

11 Make a series of cuts from the outer edge of each circle towards the center, to form petals. Carefully shape the ends of the petals with small scissors.

12 Place the smaller pink flower on top of the larger orange one and join with a few small stitches through the centers.

13 Stitch the flower decoration to the flap, hiding the back of the magnetic closure. Stitch the button in place on the flower center.

step 9

step 10

step 11

Rosie

Pink Handbag

For this version use the same yarn, Rowan Scottish Tweed Aran, but in brilliant pink 010 and felt at a higher temperature, 60°C (140°F), to make the bag slightly smaller, thicker and firmer, so there is no need to line it.

Trim the flap with a bobble braid in a bright turquoise blue and transform the clutch into a handbag with a handle made from a short length of bright turquoise blue velvet ribbon.

Eve

A big red flower looks bold and bright against a grass green border on this pretty but practical tote bag.

Materials

4 x 50 g (1¾ oz) balls Aragon Yarns Classic Romney (82 yards) in natural

2 x 50 g (1¾ oz) balls Aragon Yarns Classic Romney (82 yards) in mallard green

1 x 50 g (1¾ oz) ball Aragon Yarns Classic Romney (82 yards) in raspberry

oddment of yellow 100% wool double knitting yarn (US: worsted-weight yarn)

matching natural and green sewing threads

plastic canvas or heavy interfacing, approx. 19 x 7.5 cm (7½ x 3 in)

cotton fabric, approx. 32 x 50 cm (12½ x 19⅔ in)

Equipment

pair of 6.50 mm (US: 10½) knitting needles

tapestry needle

sewing needle

mesh laundry bag

cookie tin or rectangular object (optional)

Gauge

13 sts and 24 rows to 10 cm (4 in) over garter stitch using 6.50 (US: 10½) knitting needles

Finished size (approx.)

width: 21 cm (8¼ in)

height: 18 cm (7 in)

Method

Front and back (make 2)

1 Cast on 48 sts in natural yarn and work 66 rows in garter stitch (knit every row).

2 Break off yarn and change to mallard green. Work 20 more rows and cast off.

Sides (make 2)

3 Cast on 16 sts in natural and work 52 rows in garter stitch.

4 Break off yarn and change to mallard green. Work 20 more rows and cast off.

Handles (make 2)

5 Cast on 7 sts in mallard green and work in garter stitch until the piece measures 43 cm (17 in) in length. Cast off.

Making up

6 Stitch the cast-on rows on the front and back pieces together to form a base seam.

7 Attach the side pieces, matching the center of cast-on edges to ends of base seam. Stitch side seams. Attach handles.

step 9

Flower petals: (make 5)

8 Cast on 3 sts in raspberry yarn.
Row 1 and all odd-numbered rows: p to end.
Rows 2, 4, 6, 8 and 10: Inc in first st, k to last st, inc in last st. (13 sts)
Row 12: K to end.
Rows 14, 16 and 18: K 2 tog, k to last 2 sts, k 2 tog tbl.
Row 19: P to end. (7 sts)
Cast off.

Flower center:

9 Cast on 6 sts in yellow yarn.
Row 1 and all odd-numbered rows: P to end.
Rows 2, 4 and 6: Inc in first st, k to last st, inc in last st. (12 sts)
Row 10: K to end.
Row 12: K 2 tog, k to last 2 sts, k 2tog tbl.
Row 13: P to end.
Cast off.

10 Break off the yarn, leaving a long end. Thread this onto a tapestry needle, and thread around edge of work. Pull up and fasten off.

Felting

11 Place the flower pieces in the mesh laundry bag. Place in a washing machine along with the bag. Add detergent but no fabric softener and wash at 40°C (100°F) with no spin.

12 Pull the bag and the flower pieces gently into shape while wet and leave to dry naturally. If you wish, place a rectangular object, such as a cookie tin, inside the bag while it dries.

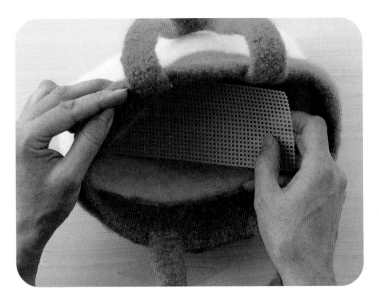

step 13

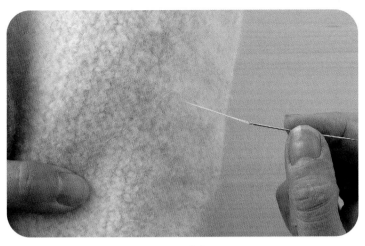

step 14

step 16

step 17

Lining

13 To line the bag, insert the rectangle of plastic canvas in the bottom of the bag to help create a firm, flat base; trim it to fit, if necessary.

14 Stitch the plastic in place in the base of the bag with a few firm stitches placed strategically at corners and at intervals along the edges.

15 Fold the lining fabric in half with the short edges together and stitch the side seams. Stitch across the two corners at the base to create a gusset.

16 Insert the lining into the bag, fold the top edges under by 2 cm (³/₄ in), pin in place, then slipstitch to the inside top of the bag, about 6 mm (¹/₄ in) down from the edge.

Finishing

17 Stitch the petals together, then stitch the flower center in place. Stitch the flower in position on the bag.

YARN TIP: The flower center requires only a small amount of yarn, so instead of buying a whole ball of yellow, use a scrap of any yarn that will felt successfully.

Stella

Wool and velvet form a luxurious partnership in this elegant handbag with chic acrylic handles. You can follow the green and pink color scheme shown here or choose your own clever combination.

Materials

4 x 50 g (1¾ oz) balls Debbie Bliss Donegal Aran Tweed (96 yards) in apple 11

30 cm (12 in) of 6 mm (¼ in) lavender velvet ribbon

2 clear pink acrylic bag handles

matching lavender and pink sewing threads

60 cm (23⅔ in) of 24 mm (1 in) pink velvet ribbon

Equipment

pair of 5.50 mm (US: 9) knitting needles

tapestry needle

sewing needle

Gauge

14 sts and 27 rows to 10 cm (4 in) measured over garter stitch using 5.50 mm (US: 9) knitting needles

Finished size (approx.)

width: 29 cm (11½ in)

height: 25 cm (10 in)

Method

Front and back (make 2)

1 Cast on 54 sts in the apple yarn. Work 9 rows in garter stitch, then dec 1 st at each end of next row. Repeat these 10 rows 7 times. (38 sts)

2 Continue in garter stitch for 16 rows without further shaping. Cast off.

Gusset (make 2)

3 Cast on 9 sts and work 96 rows in garter stitch. Cast off.

Pocket

4 Cast on 20 sts and work 32 rows in garter stitch. Cast off.

step 5

step 8

step 9

Making up

5 Stitch the pocket to the center front of the bag with a tapestry needle and spare yarn. Stitch front to back along cast-on edges. Insert gussets between front and back pieces and stitch side seams.

Felting

6 To felt, place the bag in a washing machine and wash at 40°C (100°F) with a normal powder or liquid detergent; do not use fabric softener and do not spin.

7 Remove from the machine, squeeze out excess water, pull gently into shape and leave to dry flat; do not hang up.

Finishing

8 Cut the narrow lavender velvet ribbon into four equal lengths. Slip the lengths through the slots in the bag handles and stitch both ends in place on the outside of the bag, using lavender sewing thread.

9 Stitch the pink ribbon around the top of the bag, positioning the edge of the ribbon 3 mm (⅛ in) from the top edge and slipstitching the edges to the felted fabric using matching pink sewing thread.

10 Tie a knot in the center of the remaining piece of pink ribbon, to create a simple but eye-catching detail. Fold ends under and stitch the knotted ribbon to top of pocket.

Blanche

Turquoise and green bag

Experiment with different color combinations and decorative details. This bag has been made using the same yarn in Sky 10, a soft blue-green, and partnered with clear teal handles and a lime green and pink velvet ribbon. It also features a quirky flower in a bright contrasting color, made from a small amount of red-violet double knitting wool with a center made from a circle cut from a scrap of felted fabric and gathered around the edges. The felted petals are stitched in place at the base of one of the handles and the center stitched on top.

To make the petals (make 6): cast on 4 sts using double knitting wool and 6.50 mm (US: 10½) needles.

Row 1 and all odd-numbered rows: P to end.

Row 2: Inc in first st, k 2, inc in last st.

Row 4: Inc in first st, k 4, inc in last st.

Row 6: Inc in first st, k 6, inc in last st.

Row 8: Inc in first st, k 8, inc in last st.

Next 9 rows: Work in stockinette stitch, without shaping, ending with a purl row.

Row 18: K 2 tog, k 8, k 2 tog tbl.

Row 20: K 2 tog, k 6, k 2 tog tbl. Cast off.

Place the petals in a mesh laundry bag and place in a washing machine with the bag. Wash at 40°C (100°F) with a normal powder or liquid detergent; do not use fabric sofener and do not spin.

Remove from the machine. Pull the petals gently into shape before leaving to dry.

Lisa

This small bag is the essence of chic. The fabric is firm without being bulky and the unlined interior will easily hold essentials such as make-up, phone and keys. The strap is optional and the decoration easy to achieve with a few stitches.

Materials

3 x 50 g (1¾ oz) balls Twilleys Freedom (55 yards) in ecru 401

2 skeins of DMC tapestry yarn (8¾ yards) in pale green

1 skein of DMC tapestry yarn (8¾ yards) in pale turquoise

1 skein of DMC tapestry yarn (8¾ yards) in pale yellow

2 small lobster clasps

2 small split rings

star charm and jump ring (optional)

Equipment

pair of 8.00 mm (US: 11) knitting needles

tapestry needle

knitting spool

mesh laundry bag

Gauge

11½ sts and 24 rows to 10 cm (4 in) measured over garter stitch using 8.00 mm (US: 11) knitting needles.

Finished size (approx.)

width: 22 cm (8¾ in)

height: 11 cm (4¼ in)

Method

Front and back (make 2)

1 With ecru yarn and 8.00 mm (US: 11) needles, cast on 20 sts and k 1 row.

Next 4 rows: Cast on 3 sts at beg of row, k to end.

Next 4 rows: Cast on 2 sts at beg of row, k to end.

Next 4 rows: Inc 1 st at beg of row, k to end.

Next 10 rows: Work on these 44 sts in garter stitch without further shaping.

Next row: K 18, sl 1, k 2 tog, psso, k to end.

Next row: K 16, sl 1, k 2 tog, psso, k to end.

Next row: K 14, sl 1, k 2 tog, psso, k to end.

Next row: K 12, sl 1, k 2 tog, psso, k to end.

Next row: K without further decreases.

Cast off remaining 36 sts.

SPOOL KNITTING

1 Pass the end of the yarn down through the central hole in the spool, leaving a short tail. Wind the yarn from right to left once around each nail, then on to the next in a clockwise direction.

2 Wind the yarn once round the outside of all four nails, working in a clockwise direction. Using the tapestry needle, pull the bottom loop over the top loop and off the nail.

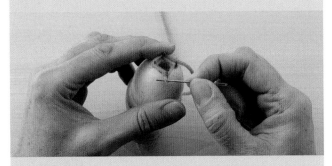

3 Continue, repeating step 2, tugging on the tail of yarn from time to time, and gradually the cord will appear through the hole in the bottom of the spool.

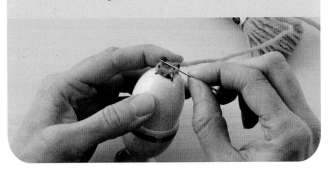

Making up

2 Stitch the front and back together along the base and sides, leaving the top open.

Handle

3 To make a cord handle, use pale green tapestry wool and the knitting spool to make a cord of the desired length (see left); it will shrink by about 10 percent once felted.

Felting

4 Place the bag in a washing machine; put the handle in the mesh laundry bag and place in the washing machine. Add detergent but no fabric conditioner and wash at 40°C (100°F) with no spin (or minimum spin).

5 Pull both bag and handle gently into shape while wet and leave to dry naturally.

Finishing

6 Using the tapestry needle and the various tapestry yarns, work rows of running stitch in pale green, pale turquoise and pale yellow. Use the picture of the finished bag as a reference.

7 Stitch a small lobster clasp to either end of the handle using the tapestry needle and a spare length of yarn.

8 Stitch a small split ring to either side of the bag and attach handle. If desired, attach a star charm to one of the rings, using a jump ring.

step 2

step 6

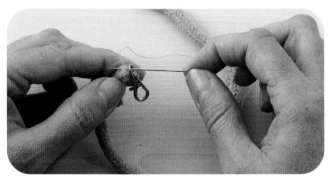

step 7

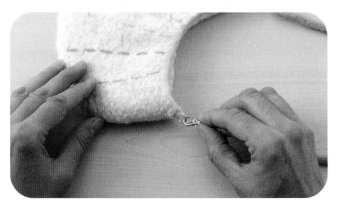

step 8

Miranda

Bag with Star motif

This bag has been made with the same yarn in Grey 421 and is decorated with a yellow felted star, which has been crocheted from one 25g ball of Jamieson & Smith 2-ply jumper-weight yarn in primrose 23, used double. For details on crochet, see pages 68–70.

To make the star: use a 6.00 mm (US: J/10) hook and double yarn to make 5 ch. Join with a sl st to form a ring.

Round 1: Work 2 ch and 9 sc in ring, join with a sl st to second of 2 ch.

Round 2: *Work 7 ch and 1 sc in second ch from hook, 1 sc in each of next 4 ch, sl st in base of ch, then sl st in each of next 2 sts; rep from * 4 times.

Round 3: Work1 sc in each st up edge of first point, 5 ch in st at top of point, 1 sc in each st down opposite side, then sl st in st between points; rep for each of remaining 4 points. Fasten off.

Stitch the felted star to the front of the bag and stitch a decorative gray button in the center.

To create a handle, use a 1.1 m (1¼ yd) length of silver-gray cord, folded in half and stitched to the inside of the bag.

Crochet

Felting adds a new dimension to simple crochet. Basic crochet stitches are easy to master, even for the beginner, and each of the crochet projects in this book is straightforward, mainly consisting of single crochet worked either in rows or, for seamless items, in rounds.

Yarns

Most pure wool yarns can be used, unless they have been treated to be easily laundered – often labeled "machine washable" or "superwash" – in which case they will not felt successfully. For crochet, yarns with a very loose twist are not particularly easy to work with as the hook tends to slip between the strands. Very hairy or fluffy yarns are also tricky as it is not easy to see individual stitches and it is therefore more difficult to know where to insert the hook.

If you wish to try out a new yarn, it is best to crochet a sample swatch and wash it in the washing machine at 40°C (100°F) to test whether it will felt or not. This will also be necessary if you want to design your own projects or adapt an existing pattern, as you will need to know not only if the yarn will felt but also how much it will shrink.

All the crochet projects in this book have clear instructions, including yarn types and quantities, so if you follow the steps carefully you will not go far wrong.

Do bear in mind, however, that felting is not an exact science and that the texture and size of your finished bag may differ slightly from the one pictured, especially if you have used a different wool. For this reason, the given dimensions of the items are approximate.

A hook and a ball of yarn are the only items you need to get started, though scissors and a tape measure will also be useful.

Hooks

The hooks used for these projects are quite large – mostly 4.00 mm (US: F/5) and 6.00 mm (US: J/10). As a general rule, items worked on the larger hooks will tend to end up slightly thicker and firmer after felting than those worked on the smaller size.

Method

Crochet

As with knitting, once the items have been made, you should secure and trim off any loose ends. Do not weave in the loose ends as this may cause lumps or uneven thickness after felting.

General tip

As a general rule, at the beginning of each row or round, a number of chain (ch) stitches are worked in place of the first stitch. This is usually 2 ch in place of 1 sc (or 3 ch in place of 1 dc, and so on). The chain stitches bring the work up to the correct height and are counted as the first stitch of the row or round. To save space, these initial chain stitches are not always specified in patterns (though in this book they are), but, with experience, it becomes second nature to include them.

Felting

Place items in a washing machine with two or three small towels or face cloths. It is better to use old towels as newer ones often shed fibers, which will become incorporated in the felt. Add normal laundry detergent but do not add fabric softener. Set the machine to a 40°C (100°F) cycle with the shortest possible spin or no spin at all.

Remember that felting sometimes produces unexpected results; you might find that items become joined together if you put too many together in the machine. Check the felted items thoroughly when you remove them from the machine to see if they have felted successfully. If stitches still look very visible or if the fabric is too soft and loose, you may need to wash the item again at a higher temperature of 60°C (140°F).

Drying

If you are happy with the texture, pull the items gently into shape while still damp and lay them out flat to dry. Do not tumble dry, as the items may become misshapen, and do not hang them up to dry as any water in the fibers can be heavy and may cause the item to stretch. You might be surprised at how long items must be left to dry, so be patient. Depending on temperature and humidity, and how dense and wet the fabric is, it can take several days or even weeks.

A foundation chain

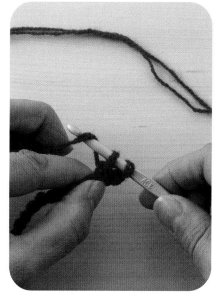
Working 1 sc into the 3rd chain

Single crochet in red and white

Kirsty

This cute little bag features stripes of varying thicknesses. Instructions are given for the pink, gray and ivory striped bag, but you can choose your own color combinations and vary the widths of the stripes.

Materials

1 x 25 g (1 oz) ball Jamieson & Smith 2-ply jumper-weight yarn (125 yards) in the following colours:

in ivory 1A

pale pink 1283

raspberry pink FC22

pale gray 203

1 or 2 small buttons

white sewing thread

Equipment

4.00 mm (US: G/6) crochet hook

tapestry needle

sewing needle

Gauge

17 sts and 15 rows to 10 cm (4 in) measured over sc using 4.00 mm (US: G/6) crochet hook

Finished size (approx.)

width: 18 cm (7 in)

height: 21 cm (8¼ in)

Method

Note that yarn is used double throughout. Work into back loop of each st.

1 Using the 4.00 mm (US: G/6) hook and two strands of ivory yarn, make 31 ch. Turn.
Round 1: Work 2 ch and 2 sc into first st, then, working along the foundation chain, 1 sc into each st to end. Work 2 sc into last st, then 1 sc into each st along the opposite side of the foundation chain. Join with sl st to first 2 ch. (64 sts)
Round 2: Remember (see page 70) that at the beginning of every round you will need to work 2 ch in place of the first sc. Work 1 sc into each st of previous round, except at either end, work 3 sc into the second of the 3 sts. Join with sl st to first 2 ch. (68 sts)
Rounds 3, 4 and 5: Repeat round 2. (80 sts)

2 Work 30 rounds of sc without further increases and changing colors every few rounds to create stripes. (Try to start each round at one of the side edges of the bag if possible.) Fasten off yarn.

Buttonhole flap

3 Find center back st and count 3 sts on either side. Rejoin gray yarn (or color used for last round) to third st to right of center and work 7 rows of sc on these 7 sts.

4 To make the button loop, 1 sc into each of first 2 sts, 4 ch, miss 3 sts, 1 sc into each of last 2 sts. Fasten off and weave the end of yarn through the sts of the last row to help create a neat button loop.

Handles

5 Count 7 sts to left of buttonhole flap. Rejoin yarn to the eighth st. Each handle is worked in rows of 3 sc; so, working on this and next 2 sts to left, work 60 rows of sc. Fasten off.

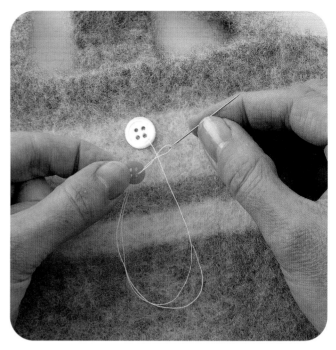

step 9

6 Leaving a gap of 7 sts between the edge of the flap and the handle, join the end of the handle to the top of the bag on the other side of the flap, using the crochet hook and sl st, or stitching in place using a tapestry needle.

7 Make a handle on the front of the bag in the same way, to match.

Felting

8 Place in a washing machine and wash at 40°C (100°F) with a normal powder or liquid detergent; do not use fabric softener and do not spin. Remove from the machine, squeeze out excess water, pull gently into shape and leave to dry flat; do not hang up.

Finishing

9 Stitch one or two buttons in place to correspond with the buttonhole. In this example, a tiny button has been stitched on top of a larger one, for decorative effect.

Nicky

Matching purse

You can use any leftover yarn to make a matching purse. Use double yarn throughout and work into back loop of each st. Using the 4.00 mm (US: G/6) hook, make 11 ch. Turn.

Round 1: Work 2 ch and 2 sc into first st, then, working along the foundation chain, 1 sc into each st to end. Now work a further 2 sc into last st, then 1 sc into each st along the opposite side of the foundation chain. Join with sl st to first 2 ch. (24 sts)

Round 2: (Remember to work 2 ch in place of the first sc at the beginning of every round, see page 70.) Work 1 sc into each st of previous round, except at either end, work 3 sc into the second of the 3 sts. Join with sl st to first 2 ch. (28 sts)

Rounds 3, 4 and 5: Repeat round 2. (40 sts)

Now work 11 rounds of sc without further increases and changing colors every few rounds to create stripes. (Try to start each round at one of the side edges of the purse.) Fasten off yarn.

To make a flap, turn and work 1 row of 20 sc. Turn.

Next row: Skip first st, work 18 sc. Turn.

Next row: Skip first st, work 16 sc. Turn.

Continue in this way, decreasing 1 st at either end of each row until you have 8 sc.

Next row (buttonhole): Skip first st, work 2 sc, 4 ch, skip 2 sts, 1 sc into each of next 2 sts. Fasten off and weave the end of the yarn through the sts of the last row, to help create a neat button loop.

Felt the purse, following the instructions given for the bag. Sew on a button.

FELTING NOTE: This yarn felts successfully at 40°C (100°F), though some shades felt more successfully at 60°C (140°F). It is advisable to felt the bag at 40°C (100°F), then remove it from the washing machine and check to see if the fabric is firm enough. You could then wash again at 60°C (140°F) if you prefer a firmer result. After felting, the fabric becomes very fluffy; if you wish, you can trim the surface with sharp scissors for a less fuzzy effect.

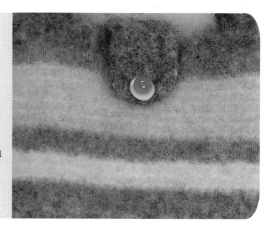

Amelie

Vertical stripes lend a quirky charm to this matching pair of practical bags. They have round bases, so they can hold a lot of "stuff."

Materials

Large bag

3 x 50 g (1¾ oz) balls Sirdar Eco Wool DK (109 yards) in ecru 200

3 x 50 g (1¾ oz) balls Sirdar Eco Wool DK (109 yards) in earth 203

Small bag

2 x 50 g (1¾ oz) balls Sirdar Eco Wool DK (109 yards)in ecru 200

2 x 50 g (1¾ oz) balls Sirdar Eco Wool DK (109 yards)in earth 203

Equipment

4.00 mm (US: G/6) crochet hook

tapestry needle

Gauge

17 sts and 15 rows to 10 cm (4 in), measured over sc using 4.00 mm (US: G/6) crochet hook

Finished size (approx.)

Large bag

height: 23 cm (9 in)

diameter: 23 cm (9 in)

Small bag

height: 18 cm (7 in)

diameter: 18 cm (7 in)

Method

Large bag

1 Using the 4.00 mm (US: G/6) hook and ecru wool, work 5 ch, join with sl st to make a ring.

Round 1: Work 2 ch and 11 sc into ring, join with sl st to second of 2 ch. (12 sts)

Round 2: Work 2 ch and 1 sc into first st, then work 2 sc into each st; join with sl st to second of 2 ch. (24 sts)

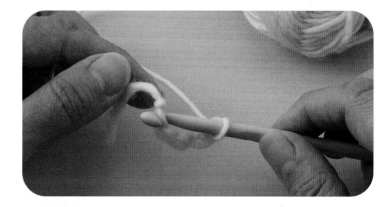

step 1

Round 3: Work in sc without any increases.

Round 4: Work 2 ch and 2 sc into next st, * sc and 2 sc into next st, then repeat from * to end; join with sl st to second of 2 ch. (36 sts)

Round 5: Work 2 ch and 1 sc into next st, 2 sc into next st, *1 sc into each of next 2 sts, 2 sc into next st, then repeat from * to end; join with sl st to second of 2 ch.

Round 6: Work in sc without any increases.

Round 7: Work 2 ch and 1 sc into each of next 2 sts, 2 sc into next st, *1 sc into each of next 3 sts, 2 sc into next st, then repeat from * to end; join with sl st to second of 2 ch.

Round 8: Work 2 ch and 1 sc into each of next 3 sts, 2 sc into next st, *1 sc into each of next 4 sts, 2 sc into next st, then repeat from * to end; join with sl st to second of 2 ch.

Round 9: Work in sc without any increases.

Round 10: Work 2 ch and 1 sc into each of next 4 sts, 2 sc into next st, *1 sc into each of next 5 sts, 2 sc into next st, then repeat from * to end; join with sl st to second of 2 ch.

Round 11: Work 2 ch and 1 sc into each of next 5 sts, 2 sc into next st, *1 sc into each of next 6 sts, 2 sc into next st, then repeat from * to end; join with sl st to second of 2 ch.

Round 12: Work in sc without any increases.

Round 13: Work 2 ch and 1 sc into each of next 6 sts, 2 sc into next st, *1 sc into each of next 7 sts, 2 sc into next st, then repeat from * to end; join with sl st to second of 2 ch.

Round 14: Work 2 ch and 1 sc into each of next 7 sts, 2 sc into next st, *1 sc into each of next 8 sts, 2 sc into next st, then repeat from * to end; join with sl st to second of 2 ch.

Round 15: Work without any increases.

Round 16: Work 2 ch and 1 sc into each of next 8 sts, 2 sc into next st, *1 sc into each of next 9 sts, 2 sc into next st, then repeat from * to end; join with sl st to second of 2 ch. (132 sts)

Round 17: Work 2 ch and 1 sc into each of next 9 sts,

step 1

2 sc into next st, *1 sc into each of next 10 sts, 2 sc into next st, then repeat from * to end; join with sl st to second of 2 ch.

Round 18: Work in sc without any increases.

Round 19: Work 2 ch and 1 sc into each of next 10 sts, 2 sc into next st, *1 sc into each of next 11 sts, 2 sc into next st, then repeat from * to end; join with sl st to second of 2 ch.

Round 20: Work 2 ch and 1 sc into each of next 11 sts, 2 sc into next st, *1 sc into each of next 12 sts, 2 sc into next st, then repeat from * to end; join with sl st to second of 2 ch. (168 sts)

Round 21: Work one round in sc without increases. Fasten off yarn.

2 For the main part of the bag, make a foundation chain of 62 ch with either the earth or ecru yarn and work in rows of sc, changing color between the ecru and earth yarn after every 2 rows to create a striped fabric. Continue until the work measures 84 cm (33 in). Stitch the two shorter sides together to form a cylinder, then stitch the circular base in place.

3 Handles (make 2): using earth yarn, make 8 ch, then join with sl st to make a ring. Work 2 ch and 1 sc into each st to end; join with sl st to second of 2 ch. Continue working in rounds to form a long tube, 60 cm (23²/₃ in) in length. Fasten off.

4 Stitch handles in place using a tapestry needle and spare yarn.

Small bag

5 To make the base, work as for large bag to end of round 16, then work 1 round of sc without increases. Fasten off.

6 For the main part of the bag, make a foundation chain of 44 ch and work in rows of sc, changing color every 2 rows to create a striped fabric. Continue until the work measures 66 cm (26 in). Stitch the two shorter sides together to form a cylinder, then stitch the circular base in place.

7 Handles (make 2): using earth yarn, make 5 ch and work in rows of sc for 62 rows. Fasten off. Stitch handles in place.

Felting

8 Place the bags in a washing machine with detergent but no fabric softener and wash at 40°C (100°F). Do not spin. Pull into shape while damp and leave to dry naturally. In order to create a round base, you can place a cookie tin or similar object inside the bag. Wait until the bag is completely dry before removing the tin.

Diane

Red-and-white-striped bag

Substitute Jamieson & Smith 2-ply jumper-weight yarn (125 yards), eight 25 g (1 oz) balls of white 1 and six 25 g (1 oz) balls of red 93. Using the yarn double throughout, follow the pattern for the larger bag, but making the handles slightly shorter – 43 cm (17 in) instead of 60 cm (23²/₃ in), or longer if you prefer. This yarn does not shrink quite so much so the resulting bag will be slightly larger. After felting, stitch a length of red bobble braid – you will need about 84 cm (33 in) – to the bag, close to the top edge.

Lily

Pastel stripes and bamboo handles make pretty touches for this very practical bag.

Materials

4 x 100 g (3½ oz) balls of knitting4fun Pure Felting Wool (219 yards) in ecru

1 x 100 g (3½ oz) ball of knitting4fun Pure Felting Wool (219 yards) in jade blue

1 x 100 g (3½ oz) ball of knitting4fun Pure Felting Wool (219 yards) in primrose

1 x 100 g (3½ oz) ball of knitting4fun Pure Felting Wool (219 yards) in pale pink

1 x 100 g (3½ oz) ball of knitting4fun Pure Felting Wool (219 yards) in lilac

4 D-rings, to fit handles

2 bamboo handles, approx. 14 cm (5½ in) diameter

matching ecru sewing thread

Equipment

6.00 mm (US: J/10) crochet hook

cookie tin or rectangular object (optional)

screwdriver

sewing needle

Gauge

15 sts and 14 rows to 10 cm (4 in) measured over sc using 6.00 mm (US: J/10) crochet hook

Finished size (approx.)

width: 24 cm (9½ in)

height: 30 cm (12 in)

Method

1 Using the 6.00 mm (US: J/10) hook and ecru yarn, work a foundation chain of 36 ch, work 2 rows of sc (with 2 ch in place of first sc of each row), then start to work in rounds on these 36 sts.

Round 1: Work 2 ch and 2 sc into first st to form a corner, work 1 sc into end of last row worked, then 3 sc into next st to form second corner; work 1 sc into each of next 34 sts (along other side of foundation ch), 3 sc into next st to form third corner, 1 sc into center of short edge, 3 sc into next st to form fourth corner, then 1 sc into each of next 34 sts; join with sl st in second of 2 ch. (82 sts)

Round 2: Work sl st into second of 3 corner sts on previous round, 2 ch and 2 sc into the same st, 1 sc into each of next 3 sts, 3 sc into corner st, 1 sc into each of next 36 sts, 3 sc into corner, 1 sc into each of next 3 sts, 3 sc into corner, then 1 sc into each of next 36 sts; join with sl st in second of 2 ch. (90 sts)

Round 3: Work sl st into second of 3 corner sts on previous round, 2 ch and 2 sc into next st, 1 sc into each of next 5 sts, 3 sc into corner st, 1 sc into each of next 38 sts, 3 sc into corner, 1 sc into each of next 5 sts, 3 sc into corner, then 1 sc into each of next 38 sts; join with sl st in second of 2 ch. (98 sts)

Work 5 more rounds in the same way, working 1 sc into each st along edges and 3 sc into each corner. (138 sts) Work a further 12 rounds without further shaping. Break off yarn.

Join in jade blue yarn and work 2 rounds. Break off yarn.

Join in ecru yarn and work 10 rounds. Break off yarn.

Join in primrose yarn and work 2 rounds. Break off yarn.

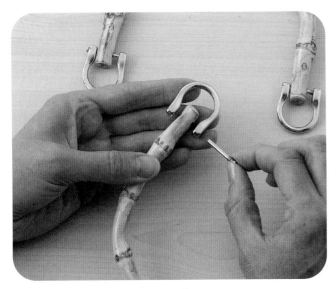

step 5

Join in pale pink yarn and work 2 rounds. Break off yarn.
Join in ecru yarn and work 10 rounds. Break off yarn.
Join in lilac yarn and work 2 rounds. Break off yarn.
Join in ecru yarn and work 10 rounds. Break off yarn.
Join in primrose yarn and work 2 rounds. Break off yarn.
Join in jade blue yarn and work 2 rounds. Break off yarn.
Join in ecru yarn and work 6 rounds. Fasten off yarn.

Handle tabs (make 4)

2 Using ecru yarn, make 6 ch. Work 24 rows of sc. Fasten off.

Felting

3 Place the bag in a washing machine; put the handle tabs in mesh laundry bag and place in the machine. Wash with normal detergent but with no fabric softener at 40°C (100°F); do not spin.

4 Pull the bag into shape while damp and leave to dry naturally; you may wish to place a cookie tin or similar object of suitable size and shape inside the bag to help create a neat rectangular shape. Leave to dry completely before removing the tin.

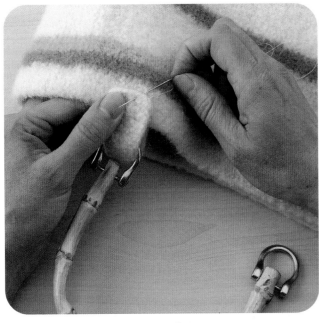

step 6

NOTE: If you wish to make a lining, lay the bag flat, measure and cut a lining from cotton fabric. Stitch the side seams, press bottom corners and stitch to make a gusset. (See page 59 for full instructions.)

Making up

5 Fix the D-rings to the bamboo handles using the screwdriver.

6 Stitch one end of each handle tab in place on the outside of the bag, positioning them to correspond with the ends of the bamboo handles. Slip a D-ring onto each and stitch the other end of each tab in place on the inside of the bag.

Grace

Textured felt bag

Combining a yarn that felts well with one that doesn't can produce interesting contrasts in texture. To make this version you will need two 50 g (1³/₄ oz) balls of Sirdar Eco Wool DK (109 yards) in ecru 200 and 1 x 50 g (1³/₄oz) ball each of Rowan Pure Wool DK in tea rose 025, lavender 039, gilt 032 and pier 006, or your choice of DK (double-knitting, or worsted-weight) yarn.

Use a 3.50 mm (US: E/44) crochet hook and follow the instructions for the main bag to end of Round 3. Continue straight as main bag, varying colored stripes by working each of the 2 rows in a different color and working the second of the 2 rows into back loop of each st. Fasten off after fourth 2-row stripe.

After felting, the colored stripes remain soft and only slightly felted.

Here, acrylic handles have been used instead of bamboo handles, but you could choose your own style, perhaps recycling handles from an old bag.

Sienna

This unusual bag is made from two felted circles with a long strap forming a gusset between them. Each piece is lined with soft cotton to make the bag more hard-wearing.

Materials

1 x 25 g (1 oz) ball Jamieson & Smith 2-ply jumper-weight yarn (125 yards) in each of the following colours:

pale turquoise 75

pale blue 14

blue FC15

lilac 49

pale pink 1283

3 x 25 g (1 oz) ball Jamieson & Smith 2-ply jumper-weight yarn (125 yards) in raspberry pink FC22

cotton fabric, at least 70 x 40 cm (27½ x 16 in)

matching pink sewing thread or invisible thread

2 buttons (optional)

Equipment

6.00 mm (US: J/10) crochet hook

sewing needle

Gauge

14 sts and 13 rows to 10 cm (4 in) measured over sc using 6.00 mm (US: J/10) crochet hook and double yarn

Finished size (approx.)

diameter: 23 cm (9 in)

depth: 5 cm (2 in)

Method

Note that the yarn is used double throughout.

Front and back (make 2)

1 Using the 6.00 mm (US: J/10) hook and two strands of pale turquoise yarn, work 5 ch, join with sl st to make a ring.

Round 1: Work 2 ch and 11 sc into ring; join with sl st to second of 2 ch. (12 sts)

Round 2: Work 2 ch and 1 sc into first st, then work 2 sc into each st; join with sl st to second of 2 ch. (24 sts)

Round 3: Work 2 ch and 2 sc into next st, *1 sc into next st, 2 sc into next st, then repeat from * to end; join with sl st to second of 2 ch. (36 sts)

Round 4: Work in sc without any increases. Break off yarn and join in pale blue yarn.

Round 5: Work 2 ch and 1 sc into next st, 2 sc into next st, *1 sc into each of next 2 sts, 2 sc into next st, then repeat from * to end; join with sl st to second of 2 ch. (48 sts)

Round 6: Work 2 ch and 1 sc into each of next 2 sts, 2 sc into next st, *1 sc into each of next 3 sts, 2 sc into next st, then repeat from * to end; join with sl st to second of 2 ch. (60 sts)

Round 7: Work in sc without increases. Break off yarn and join in blue yarn.

Round 8: Work 2 ch and 1 sc into each of next 3 sts, 2 sc into next st, *1 sc into each of next 4 sts, 2 sc into next st, then repeat from * to end; join with sl st to second of 2 ch. (72 sts)

step 1

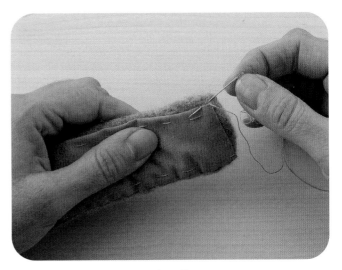

step 5

Round 9: Work 2 ch and 1 sc into each of next 4 sts, 2 sc in next st, *1 sc in each of next 5 sts, 2 sc in next st, then repeat from * to end; join with sl st to second of 2 ch. (84 sts)

Round 10: Work in sc without increases. Break off yarn and join in lilac.

Round 11: Work 2 ch and 1 sc into each of next 5 sts, 2 sc into next st, *1 sc into each of next 6 sts, 2 sc into next st, then repeat from * to end; join with sl st to second of 2 ch. (96 sts)

Round 12: Work 2 ch and 1 sc into each of next 6 sts, 2 sc into next st, *1 sc into each of next 7 sts, 2 sc into next st, then repeat from * to end; join with sl st to second of 2 ch. Break off yarn and join in pale pink. (108 sts)

Round 13: Work in sc without increases.

Round 14: Work 2 ch and 1 sc into each of next 7 sts, 2 sc into next st, *1 sc into each of next 8 sts, 2 sc into next st, then repeat from * to end; join with sl st to second of 2 ch. Break off yarn and join in raspberry pink. (120 sts)

Round 15: Work 2 ch and 1 sc into each of next 8 sts, 2 sc into next st, *1 sc into each of next 9 sts, 2 sc into next st, then repeat from * to end; join with sl st to second of 2 ch. (132 sts)

Round 16: Work in sc without increases.

Round 17: Work 2 ch and 1 sc into each of next 9 sts, 2 sc into next st, *1 sc into each of next 10 sts, 2 sc into next st, then repeat from * to end; join with sl st to second of 2 ch. (144 sts)

Round 18: Work 2 ch and 1 sc into each of next 10 sts, 2 sc into next st, *1 sc into each of next 11 sts, 2 sc into next st, then repeat from * to end; join with sl st to second of 2 ch. (156 sts)

Round 19: Work in sc without increases. Fasten off yarn.

Strap

2 Make 12 ch and work 120 rows of sc or until the work measures desired length, allowing for about 20–25% shrinkage.

Felting

3 Place the circles and the strap in a washing machine and wash at 40°C (100°F) with a normal powder or liquid detergent; do not use fabric softener and do not spin.

4 Remove from the machine, squeeze out excess water, pull gently into shape and lay out flat to dry; do not hang up.

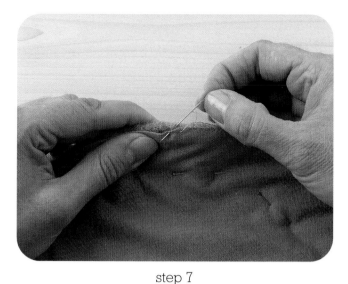

step 7

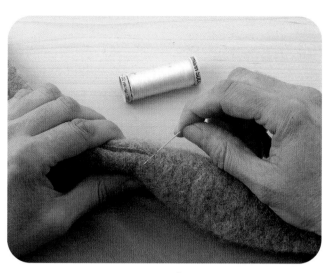

step 8

Making up

5 To make the lining, cut a strip of the cotton fabric 2 cm (¾ in) longer and 2 cm (¾ in) wider than the strap, joining pieces if necessary to obtain the right length, and cut two circles with a diameter 2 cm (¾ in) wider than the front and back.

6 Turn under 1 cm (½ in) all round the strap lining and slipstitch the folded edge to the edges of the strap using pink sewing thread.

7 Pin one circle of fabric lining to each of the two felted circles, then turn under the raw edge, slipstitching the fold to the edge of the felted circle as you go.

8 Now join the lined components, placing lined sides together and using either pink sewing thread or invisible thread, overstitching the edges of the felted fabric. Start with one end of the strap, which will be at the base of the finished bag, and leave a 15 cm (6 in) opening at center top of bag.

9 If desired, stitch two decorative buttons, one on top of the other, in the center of bag front.

NOTE: Even after felting, there may be a small hole in the center of the circles that form the front and back of the bag. Here, two small buttons have been used to cover a small hole at the front. Search your button box for odd buttons that match the colors of the yarns, or use a brooch or other decoration of your choice.

Fleur

With its floral decorations and spacious interior, this bag is both attractive and practical.

Materials

4 x 50 g (1¾ oz) balls Jamieson & Smith soft-spun yarn (98 yards) in damson 9

4 x 50 g (1¾ oz) balls Jamieson & Smith soft-spun yarn (98 yards) in teal green 19

2 m (78¾ in) of 1 cm (½ in) thick cord

5 cm (2 in) length of 3 cm (1¼ in) wide tape

1 x 25 g (1 oz) ball Jamieson & Smith 2-ply jumper-weight yarn (125 yards) in raspberry pink FC22

1 x 25 g (1 oz) ball Jamieson & Smith 2-ply jumper-weight yarn (125 yards) in bright turquoise 132

1 x 25 g (1 oz) ball Jamieson & Smith 2-ply jumper-weight yarn (125 yards) in white 1

matching white sewing thread

small amount of white fleece

2 x 32 mm (1¼ in) buttons

Equipment

6.00 mm (US: J/10) crochet hook

tapestry needle

mesh laundry bag

Gauge

14 sts and 13 rows to 10 cm (4 in) measured over sc using 6.00 mm (US: J/10) crochet hook

Finished size (approx.)

width: 36 cm (14¼ in)

height: 32 cm (12½ in)

Method

1 With the 6.00 mm (US: J/10) hook and damson yarn, make 20 ch.

Round 1: Work 2 ch and 5 sc into first ch, then, working along the foundation chain, 1 sc into each of next 18 ch. Now work 6 sc into last ch, then 1 sc into each st along the opposite side of the foundation ch. Join with sl st to second of 2 ch. (48 sts)

Round 2: (Remember to work to work 2 ch in place of the first sc at the beginning of every round, see page 70). Work 2 sc into each of next 6 sts, 1 sc into each of next 18 sts, 2 sc into each of next 6 sts, then 1 sc into each of next 18 sts; join with sl st to second of 2 ch. (60 sts)

Round 3: Work 2 ch and 1 sc into each st to end; join with sl st to second of 2 ch.

Round 4: Work 2 ch and 2 sc into next st, [1 sc into next st, 2 sc into next st] 5 times, 1 sc into each of next 18 sts, [1 sc into next st, 2 sc into next st] 6 times, then 1 sc into each of next 18 sts; join with sl st to second of 2 ch. (72 sts)

Round 5: Work 2 ch and 1 sc into each st to end; join with sl st to second of 2 ch.

Round 6: Work 2 ch and 1 sc into next st, 2 sc into next st, [1 sc into next 2 sts, 2 sc into next st] 5 times, 1 sc in each of next 18 sts, [1 sc into next 2 sts, 2 sc into next st] 6 times, then 1 sc into each of next 18 sts; join with sl st to second of 2 ch. (84 sts)

Round 7: Work 2 ch and 1 sc into each st to end; join with sl st to second of 2 ch.

Round 8: Work 2 ch and 1 sc into next 2 sts, 2 sc into next st, [1 sc into next 3 sts, 2 sc into next st] 5 times, 1 sc into each of next 18 sts, [1 sc into next 3 sts, 2 sc into next st] 6 times, then 1 sc into each of next 18 sts; join with sl st to second of 2 ch. (96 sts)

step 12

Round 9: Work 2 ch and 1 sc into each st to end; join with sl st to second of 2 ch.

Round 10: Work 2 ch and 1 sc into next 3 sts, 2 sc in next st, [1 sc into next 4 sts, 2 sc into next st] 5 times, 1 sc into each of next 18 sts, [1 sc into next 4 sts, 2 sc into next st] 6 times, then 1 sc into each of next 18 sts; join with sl st to second of 2 ch. (108 sts)

Round 11: Work 2 ch and 1 sc into each st to end; join with sl st to second of 2 ch.

Round 12: Work 2 ch and 1 sc into next 4 sts, 2 sc in next st, [1 sc into next 5 sts, 2 sc into next st] 5 times, 1 sc into each of next 18 sts, [1 sc into next 5 sts, 2 sc into next st] 6 times, then 1 sc into each of next 18 sts; join with sl st to second of 2 ch. (120 sts)

2 Work 24 rounds of sc (2 ch, then 1 sc into each st to end).
Next round: Work 2 ch and 1 sc into each of next 9 sts, 2 sc tog, *1 sc into each of next 10 sts, 2 sc tog, then rep from * to end; join with sl st to second of 2 ch. (110 sts)
Next round: Work 2 ch and 1 sc into each of next 8 sts, 2 sc tog, *1 sc into each of next 9 sts, 2 sc tog, rep from * to end; join with sl st to second of 2 ch. (100 sts) Fasten off yarn.

3 Join in teal green yarn and work 20 rounds of sc with no further shaping.
Next round: Work 2 ch and 1 sc into each of next 20 sts, turn and work 10 rows of 6 sc to create first tab; break yarn and rejoin to top edge of bag, next to base of tab, and work 1 sc into each of next 50 sts; turn and work 10 rows of 6 sc to create second tab; break yarn and rejoin to top edge of bag, next to base of second tab, and work 1 sc into each of next 29 sts to end; join with sl st to second of 2 ch. Fasten off yarn.

4 Turn over the top 2 rows to the inside of the bag and, using the tapestry needle and a length of matching yarn, stitch to form a narrow hem; the tabs will be inside bag.

Handle

5 To make a tube for the handle make 12 ch using teal green yarn and join with sl st to first ch to form a ring.
Round 1: Work 2 ch and 1 sc into each of next 11 ch; join with sl st to second of 2 ch.
Repeat last round 47 times; fasten off yarn.

Large petals (make 5)

6 With the 6.00 mm (US: J/10)hook and two strands of raspberry pink yarn, make 3 ch and 2 sc into last ch; turn.
Row 1: Work 2 ch and 1 sc into first st, 1 sc into next st, then 2 sc into last st; turn. (5 sts)
Row 2: Work 2 ch and 1 sc into first st, 1 sc into each of next 3 sts, then 2 sc into last st; turn. (7 sts)
Row 3: Work 2 ch, 1 sc into first st, 1 sc in each of next 5 sts, then 2 sc into last st; turn. (9 sts)
Rows 4, 5, 6 and 7: work 4 rows of sc.
Row 8: Work 2 ch and 2 sc tog, 1 sc into each of next 3 sts, 2 sc tog, then 1 sc into last st. (7 sts)
Row 9: Work 2 ch and 2 sc tog, 1 sc into next st, 2 sc tog, then 1 sc into last st. (5 sts)
Row 10: Work 2 ch and 3 sc tog, then 1 sc into last st. Fasten off.

Small petals (make 5)

7 With the 6.00 mm (US: J/10)hook and two strands of raspberry pink yarn, make 3 ch and 2 sc into last ch; turn.
Row 1: Work 2 ch and 1 sc in first st, 1 sc into next st, then 2 sc into last st; turn. (5 sts)

Row 2: Work 2 ch and 1 sc in first st, 1 sc into each of next 3 sts, then 2 sc into last st; turn. (7 sts)

Rows 3, 4 and 5: Work 3 rows of sc.

Row 6: Work 2 ch and 2 sc tog, 1 sc into next st, 2 sc tog, then 1 sc into last st. (5 sts)

Row 7: Work 2 ch and 3 sc tog, then 1 sc into last st. Fasten off yarn.

Leaves (make 6)

8 With 6.00 mm (US: J/10) hook and two strands of bright turquoise yarn, make 3 ch and 2 sc into last ch; turn.

Row 1: Work 2 ch and 1 sc into first st, then 1 sc into each st to end; turn.

Rows 2, 3, 4 and 5: Repeat last row 4 times. (8 sts)

Row 6: Work 1 row of sc.

Row 7: Work 2 ch and 1 sc into each of next 5 sts, then 2 sc tog. (7 sts)

Row 8: Work 2 ch and 1 sc into each of next 4 sts, then 2 sc tog. (6 sts)

Row 9: Work 2 ch and 1 sc into each of next 3 sts, then 2 sc tog. (5 sts)

Row 10: Work 2 ch and 1 sc into each of next 2 sts, then 2 sc tog. (4 sts)

Row 11: Work 2 ch and 1 sc into next st, then 2 sc tog. (3 sts)

Row 12: Work 2 ch and 2 sc tog. Fasten off yarn.

Flower centers (make 2)

9 Using two strands of white yarn, wind the yarn around your finger to make a ring and, using the 6.00 mm (US: J/10) hook, work 2 ch and 5 sc into ring, join with sl st to second of 2 ch and pull the ends of the yarn to close up the hole in the center.

Round 1: Work 2 ch and 1 sc into first st, then work 2 sc into next 5 sts; join with sl st to second of 2 ch. (12 sts)

Round 2: Work 2 ch and 2 sc into next st, *1 sc into next st, 2 sc into next st, then repeat from * to end; join with sl st to second of 2 ch. (18 sts)

Round 3: Work 2 ch and 1 sc into next st, 2 sc into next st,

*1 sc into each of next 2 sts, 2 sc into next st, then repeat from * to end; join with sl st to second of 2 ch. Fasten off.

Felting

10 Place the bag and the handle in the washing machine and place the smaller components in a mesh laundry bag in the machine. Wash at 40°C (100°F) with a normal powder or liquid detergent; do not use fabric softener and do not spin.

11 Remove from machine, squeeze out excess water, pull gently into shape and leave to dry; do not hang up.

Making up

12 Join the ends of the cord by stitching them together and binding with tape. Try not to make the join too bulky but do not worry if the stitching is not neat as the join will be covered by the felted tube handle.

13 Slip the felted tube over the double thickness of cord and secure in place with a few discreet stitches.

14 Fold each felted tab on the top edge of the bag over one strand of the cord handle and stitch in place on the outside of the bag using the tapestry needle and matching yarn.

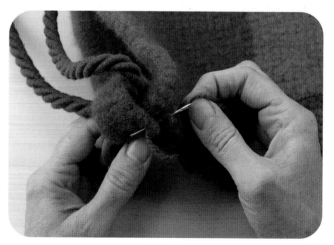

step 14

15 Stitch a gathering thread around the edge of each of the flower centers using white sewing thread. Place a little fleece in the center of each circle to pad it out, then add a button to give it a nice round shape. Finally, pull up the gathering thread tightly and secure firmly.

16 Make up the flowers. First stitch the five large petals together to form a flower and stitch the ends of four of the leaves to the center of the back of the flower. Join the smaller flower petals together and add the remaining two leaves.

17 Stitch both of the flowers on the bag front, below each of the handles. (Note: if you find it easier, stitch the leaves to the bag first then stitch each flower petal in place directly on to the bag.) Finally, stitch the flower centers in place.

step 15

step 17

NOTE: Two flowers make a bold statement, but you may wish to make several more flowers, maybe in a variety of colors to create a multi-colored flower border. Be creative!

Lucy

This practical holdall is plain and understated, with small discs of color forming a decorative feature at the base of each handle.

Materials

4 x 50 g (1¾ oz) balls of Jamieson & Smith 2-ply jumper-weight yarn (125 yards) in natural undyed 2001

1 x 25 g (1 oz) ball of Jamieson & Smith 2-ply jumper-weight yarn (125 yards) in heather FC51

4 pearl buttons, 3 cm (1¼ in) in diameter

matching lilac sewing thread

Equipment

6.00 mm (US: J/10) crochet hook

tapestry needle

sewing needle

mesh laundry bag

Gauge

13 sts and 11 rows to 10 cm (4 in) measured over sc using 6.00 mm (US: J/10) crochet hook and double yarn

Finished size (approx.)

width: 33 cm (13 in)
height: 31 cm (12¼ in)

Method

Note that yarn is used double throughout.

Front and back (make 2)

1 With 6.00 mm (US: J/10) hook and 2 strands of natural undyed yarn, make 60 ch.

Row 1: Work 2 ch in first ch, then work 1 sc into each ch to end. (60 sts)

Repeat previous row 9 times.

Row 11: Work 2 ch, 2 sc tog and 1 sc into each st to last 3 sts; 2 sc tog and 1 sc in last st.

Work 8 rows in sc without shaping.

Row 20: As row 11.

Work 8 rows in sc without shaping.

Row 29: As row 11.

Work 8 rows in sc without shaping.

Row 38: As row 11.

Work 8 rows in sc without shaping.

Fasten off.

Handles (make 2)

2 With 6.00 mm (US: J/10) hook and 2 strands of natural undyed yarn, make 7 ch.

Row 1: Work 2 ch and 1 sc into each ch to end. (7 sts)

Repeat previous row 119 times.

Fasten off.

Discs (make 4)

3 Using 2 strands of heather yarn, loop the yarn around your finger to make a ring and, with the 6.00 mm (US: J/10) hook, work 2 ch and 9 sc into the loop; join with a sl st to second of 2 ch and pull the ends of the yarn to close up the hole in the center.

Next round: Work 2 ch and 1 sc into first st, then 2 sc into each st to end; join with sl st to second of 2 ch.

Next round: Work 2 ch and 2 sc into next st, *1 sc into next st, 2 sc into next st, then rep from * to end; join with sl st to second of 2 ch.

Fasten off.

step 2

step 3

Making up

4 Stitch the front to the back along the foundation chains and side seams using the tapestry needle and matching yarn.

5 Stitch handles in place on front and back, positioning the ends about a third of the way up from the base.

Felting

6 Place the bag in a washing machine. Put the handles and discs in a mesh laundry bag and also place in the machine. Wash at 40°C (100°F) with a powder or liquid detergent; do not use fabric softener and do not spin.

7 Remove from the machine, squeeze out excess water and pull gently into shape. Lay out on a flat surface and leave to dry; do not hang up.

Finishing

8 Using lilac thread and the sewing needle, stitch the discs over the ends of the four handle joins. Sew a button in the center of each disc.

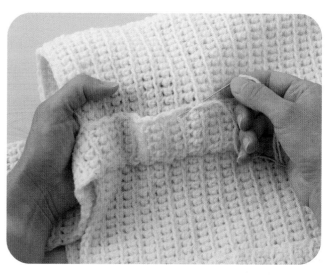

step 5

NOTE: When joining pieces of crochet (or knitting) prior to felting, it is best to use spare yarn as this will shrink and become integrated into the finished bag. When stitching pieces together after felting, however, or when adding buttons and other decorative or functional pieces, it is advisable to use sewing thread in a color to match the felted fabric, as this will become embedded in the fabric and will therefore be fairly discreet and unnoticeable.

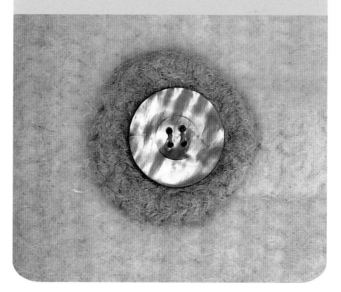

Recycling

Most of us have personal experience of the irreversible process of washing a wool sweater at the wrong temperature, resulting in an unwearable garment a fraction of its original size. But, as the techniques and projects in previous chapters demonstrate, shrinking wool fabric can produce exciting and attractive results.

A quick way to produce a felted bag is to take an existing woolen item – even one that has been nibbled by moths – and deliberately shrinking it in a washing machine, then constructing the bag from the resulting felted fabric.

Unwanted knits such as sweaters, scarves and blankets can be made into felted items, giving them a whole new lease of life. Patterned knits can work just as well as plain ones. Check cupboards and drawers, or visit garage sales and thrift stores for suitable items – even those with signs of damage or wear. Any holes and stains can be cut away and the components for a bag cut from the best bits of the fabric.

Moths are a pest as far as any wool fabrics are concerned. If your old sweater has been attacked by moths, wait and see how it turns out after it has been felted in the washing machine. Tiny holes often miraculously disappear as the fabric shrinks, while larger holes can be positioned in such a way that they can be covered up or disguised with a pocket or motif. You could also try darning any substantial holes before or after felting, using a matching yarn.

Method

Preparation

If you wish, you can dismantle garments before felting (rather than placing the whole item in the washing machine) as you may find it easier to handle smaller pieces. It is also often easier to cut through knitted fabrics before they have been felted. Cut off sleeves and cut away and discard the seams as you will only be using the flat areas of fabric. You may wish to discard button bands and ribbing, too, though these can sometimes be very useful for making straps and handles.

Felting

As with knitted and crocheted projects, recycled fabrics can be felted in a washing machine. Try a 40°C (100°F) wash at first, with a normal detergent, either powder or liquid, and no fabric softener. Set the machine for a minimum spin or, preferably, no spin at all. If the item does not felt to your satisfaction, try again at 60°C (140°F).

Drying

When the items emerge from the washing machine dripping wet, gently squeeze out excess water and lay the item flat. If this is not practical – for large items such as blankets, for example – you can drape them over a washing line or suspend them from a pole over the bath; but do not use any pegs, as they will leave dents in the fabric.

Check before the felted fabric is completely dry: if it is very creased, you may need to steam it. Use a hand-held steamer or steam iron to remove creases before cutting out your pattern pieces and assembling your bag, as creases will be more difficult to remove once the bag has been made.

Cutting and stitching

Templates for the some of the bags are on pages 106–109. Some of these need to be enlarged; you could do this using a photocopier or by copying them onto graph paper. Mark out pattern shapes on felted fabric using a ruler and tailor's chalk or erasable fabric pen and cut out the pattern pieces using a good pair of sharp dressmaking scissors. Pin fabric pieces together using glass-headed pins, which are less likely to get lost in the thick woolen fibers. Components can be stitched together by hand or using a sewing machine. Felted fabric doesn't fray when cut so seams can be on the outside of the bag; this also reduces unnecessary bulk.

Felted fabric provides an excellent surface for appliqué and embroidery. In most cases, you will find that your needle glides through the fabric. Blunt tapestry needles can be used for some fabric, though a thick, long sharp needle with a large eye is the best all-round choice for joining seams and adding embroidery stitches.

Martha

This practical shoulder bag uses pieces cut from a striped sweater and has flowers attached by needle felting. The pattern makes use of the sweater's ribbed bands for the strap but if your sweater doesn't have any you can use strips from the body or sleeves instead.

Materials

striped wool sweater

matching blue sewing thread

small amounts of merino wool tops in blue, ivory, yellow and bright pink

Equipment

ruler

tailor's chalk or erasable fabric pen

sewing needle

sewing machine (optional)

foam block, about 28 cm (11 in) wide

felting needle

Finished size (approx.)

width: 23 cm (9 in)

height: 27 cm (10 $^2/_3$ in)

depth: 6 cm (2$^1/_2$ in)

Method

Felting

1 Remove any buttons or other fastenings and either place the whole sweater in the washing machine or cut off the sleeves and cut away and discard the seams before placing the pieces in the washing machine. Wash at 40°C (100°F) with a normal powder or liquid detergent; do not use fabric softener and do not spin.

2 Remove from the machine, squeeze out excess water, pull gently into shape and leave to dry. Once dry, cut off the sleeves and cut away and discard the seams if you have not done so already. If the felted fabric is creased, press with a steam iron.

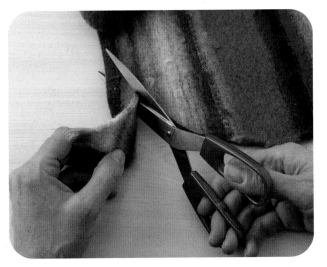

step 2

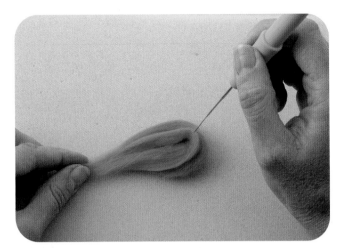

step 8

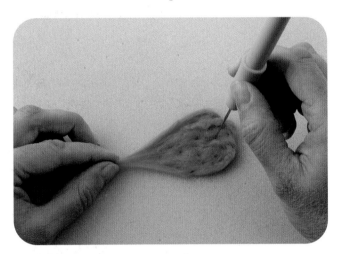

step 9

step 10

Making up

3 Cut off the ribbed bands from the sweater and reserve. Using a ruler and tailor's chalk or erasable fabric pen, measure rectangles for the front, back, base and sides of the bag in the following measurements:
Front: 28 x 24 cm (11 x 9½ in)
Side pieces (make 2): 28 x 7 cm (11 x 2¾ in)
Base: 24 x 7 cm (9½ x 2¾ in)
Back (includes the flap): 42 x 24 cm (16½ x 9½ in)
Cut out the rectangles.

4 Stitch one narrow end of each side piece to the base, followed by one of the shorter ends of both the back and front, then stitch the side seams. This can be done by hand or machine; make sure you have wrong sides of all pieces facing inwards as the seams will be on the outside of the finished bag.

5 Cut a strap approximately 3 cm (1¼ in) wide and 78 cm (30¾ in) long from the ribbed band of the sweater. Stitch the ends to the side pieces of the bag, on the inside.

6 Cut the bag flap into a shape, such as a semicircle or triangle, or leave as a rectangle if you prefer.

Flowers

7 To make the petals, pull out a bunch of blue fibers from the hank and loop them over your finger; this makes a single petal.

8 Place the fibers on a foam block and needle felt by pricking them with the end of the felting needle using rapid stabbing motions. Keep the needle in a vertical position as you work, or the needle may snap. From time to time, lift and turn the piece so that it does not become too firmly embedded in the foam. Needle felt until quite firm and well bonded, turning frequently.

9 Continue with this process until the fibers are firm and hold together. Repeat to make 10 petals in all.

step 14

10 Join 5 petals to make a flower by overlapping them slightly and continuing to prick with the felting needle until the fibers are bonded together. Repeat with the other 5 petals to make another flower.

11 Twist white fibers to make two circles and needle felt these into the center of each flower. Twist pink fibers into smaller circles to make flower centers.

Finishing

12 Place the foam block inside the bag, position one of the flowers on the bag front (with the foam directly underneath) and use the felting needle to attach them to the bag. Twist small wisps of yellow fibers to make stamens and place one on each petal, then felt in place. Continue stabbing with the needle until the fibers have bonded to the fabric and are visible on the reverse side.

13 Repeat with the second flower, positioning it on the edge of the flap, slightly overhanging. For added security, stitch the edges of the flowers to the bag using matching thread and tiny stitches.

14 Stitch the ends of the bag handle in place on the inside of the bag.

NEEDLE FELTING

Without water or soap, this dry felting technique uses special barbed needles to tangle fibers into a dense fabric. It is a useful way of bonding decorations to larger pieces. Needle-felted decorations can be added to wet-felted, knitted or crocheted fabrics, or to a range of fabrics, including denim and velvet.

The essential equipment includes felting needles, a foam pad and carded fibers. For this project, a single felting needle is all you need, but for making larger pieces, you may like to try using a multi-needle tool.

NOTE: If the felted fabric is very soft and stretchy, you may wish to line the bag. You can make up the lining from your chosen fabric in the same way as the main bag. Slip the lining inside the bag, wrong sides together, fold the top edge to the inside and slipstitch in place.

Caroline

This cute yet stylish bag started life as a wool blanket. It's just the right size for a toiletries bag, nightie and a change of underwear.

Materials

pale pink wool blanket

piece of blue ready-made wool-viscose felt, at least 24 x 12 cm (9½ x 4¾ in)

piece of lilac ready-made wool-viscose felt, at least 24 x 12 cm (9½ x 4¾ in)

matching pale pink, blue and lilac sewing threads

48 cm (19 in) zip

heavyweight interfacing, 32 x 11 cm (12½ x 4¼ in)

4 x D-rings, 3.5 cm (1⅓ in) wide

2 x buckles, 3.5 cm (1⅓ in) wide

Equipment

ruler

tailor's chalk or erasable fabric pen

sewing needle

sewing machine (optional)

Finished size (approx.)

width: 36 cm (14¼ in)

height: 24 cm (9½ in)

depth: 12 cm (4¾ in)

Method

Felting

1 Place the blanket in the washing machine. Wash at 40°C (100°F) with a powder or liquid detergent; do not use fabric softener and do not spin.

2 Remove from the machine, squeeze out excess water, pull gently into shape and leave to dry. Once dry, if the felted fabric is creased, press with a steam iron.

Making up

3 Using the template on page 108, mark and cut out two trapezoids to make the front and back of the bag.

4 Measure out rectangles with the following measurements using a ruler and tailor's chalk or erasable fabric pen:

Top (make 2): 52 x 6 cm (20½ x 2½ in)

Base and sides (1 piece): 66 x 12 cm (26 x 4¾ in)

Tabs (make 4): 6 x 2.5 cm (2½ x 1 in)

Handles (make 2): 32 x 2.5 cm (12½ x 1 in)

Cut these out.

step 5

step 6

5 Trace the flower motifs from page 108 and use them to cut shapes from the blue and lilac ready-made felt.

6 Pin the flower and leaf shapes to the front piece of the bag and attach by stitching by hand or machine, with close zigzag or satin stitch, around the edge of each motif using matching sewing thread.

7 Stitch the zip between the two top pieces of the bag.

8 Place the piece of interfacing in the center of the base of the bag and stitch in place.

9 Pin and baste the base to the front and back pieces, followed by the top piece with the zip.

10 Insert a tab into each D-ring, fold the tab double and insert the ends into the top seams, pinning in place. Overlap the ends of the base piece over the ends of the top where they meet at the sides, and pin.

11 Stitch the seams by hand or machine, with the seams on the outside.

12 Slip one end of one of the handles into the left-hand D-ring on the front of the bag, fold over about 2.5 cm (1 in) and stitch through both thicknesses to secure. Slip the other end through a buckle, through the D-ring and back through the buckle. Repeat with the other handle on the back of the bag. The length of the handles can now be adjusted.

Edith

This lively shoulder bag is made from a single sweater. Decorated with a heart appliqué, it is edged with colorful blanket stitch.

Materials

plain blue wool sweater

scrap of red felted fabric at least 13 x 13 cm (5 x 5 in)

2 skeins of DMC tapestry yarn in hot pink 8456

matching blue sewing thread

1.2 m (1⅓ yd) of 28 mm (1 in) wide blue ribbon

Equipment

ruler

tailor's chalk or erasable fabric pen

large embroidery needle

sewing needle

sewing machine (optional)

Finished size (approx.)

width: 23 cm (9 in)

height: 27 cm (10⅔ in)

step 5

step 6

Method

Felting

1 Remove buttons or other fastenings and either place the whole sweater in the washing machine or cut off the sleeves and cut away and discard the seams before placing the pieces in the washing machine. Wash at 40°C (100°F) with a normal powder or liquid detergent; do not use fabric softener and do not spin.

2 Remove from the machine, and squeeze out any excess water. Pull gently into shape and leave to dry.

3 Once dry, cut off the sleeves and cut away and discard the seams if you have not done so already. If the felted fabric is creased, press with a steam iron.

Making up

4 Cut off the ribbed bands from the sweater and reserve. Measure rectangles for the front, back, base and sides of the bag using a ruler and tailor's chalk or erasable fabric pen with the following measurements:
Front and back (make 2): 28 x 24 cm (11 x 9½ in)
Side pieces (make 2): 28 x 7 cm (11 x 2¾ in)
Base: 24 x 7 cm (9½ x 2¾ in)
Cut out the rectangles.

5 Trace the heart motif from page 109 and use it to cut a shape from the piece of red felted fabric.

6 Pin the felt heart to the center of the front piece of the bag and attach by stitching it with an embroidery needle and tapestry yarn, in blanket stitch, around the edge of the motif.

7 Stitch one narrow end of each side piece to the base, followed by one of the shorter ends of both the back

step 9

and front, then stitch the side seams. This can be done by hand or machine; make sure you have wrong sides of all pieces facing inwards as the seams will be on the outside of the finished bag.

8 Cut a strap from the ribbed band of the sweater approximately 3 cm (1¼ in) wide and 120 cm (47¼ in) long, joining pieces if necessary to obtain the right length. Stitch the ribbon to one side of the strap, to reinforce it and to prevent it stretching in use. Stitch the ends of the strap to the side pieces of the bag, on the inside.

9 Finish the seams and top edge of the bag with blanket stitch.

Templates

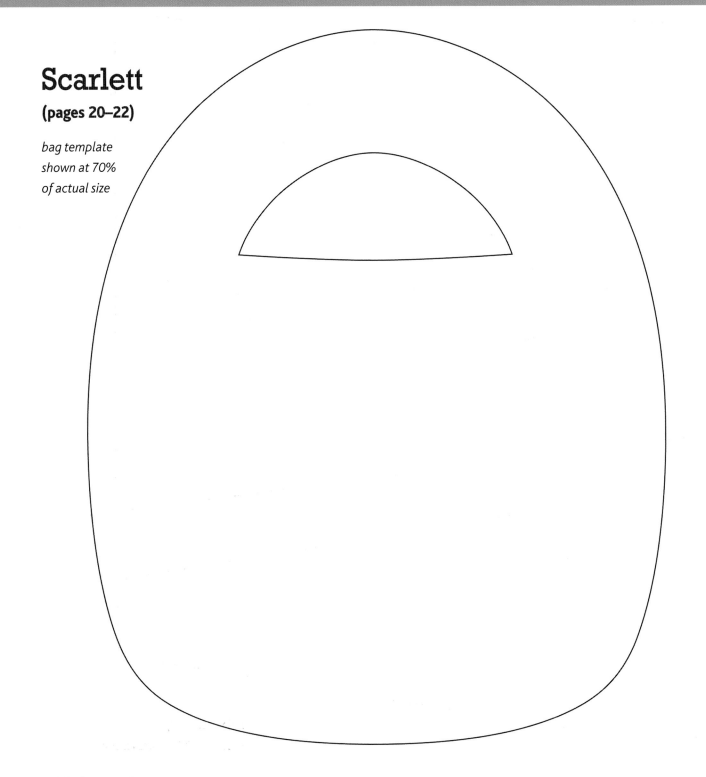

Scarlett

(pages 20–22)

*bag template
shown at 70%
of actual size*

Emma

(pages 32–35)

Front and back (make 2) and flower design
shown at 50% of actual size

Sides (make 2)
shown at 50% of actual size

Caroline

(pages 100–102)

Front and back (make 2)
shown at 50% of size

Flower motifs
shown at 50% of size

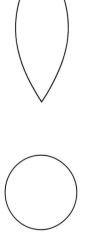

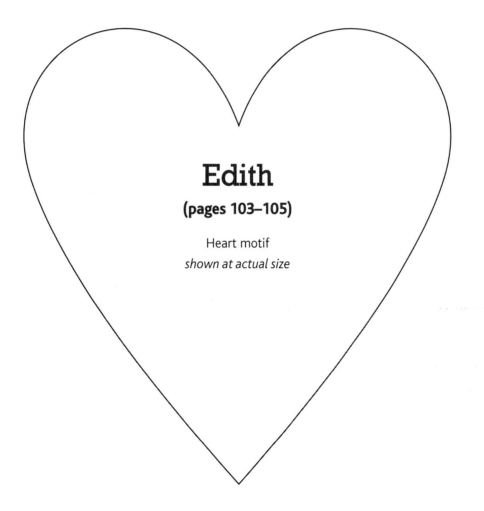

Edith

(pages 103–105)

Heart motif
shown at actual size

Resources

Wool Tops, Other Fibers, and Felting Needles

Fascinations Fiber Gallery & Studio
211 Bannister, Suite 9A
Plainwell, MI 49080
Tel: (269) 685-7077
www.hookedonfelt.com

Halcyon Yarn
12 School Street
Bath, ME 04530
Tel: (800) 341-0282
www.halcyonyarn.com

Marr Haven Wool Farm
772 39th Street
Allegan, MI 49010-9353
Tel: (269) 673-8800
www.marrhaven.com

Morehouse Farm/Sheep's Clothing
2 Rock City Road
Milian, NY 12571
Tel: (845) 758-3710
www.morehousefarm.com

Outback Fibers from The Wool Shed
312 Oak Plaza Cove
Georgetown, TX 78628
Tel: (800) 276-5015
www.outbackfibers.com

Paradise Fibers
3353 East Trent Avenue
Spokane, WA 99202
Tel: (509) 599-6986
www.paradisefibers.com

The Spinster's Treadle
1640 Tyrone Road
Morgantown, WV 26508
Tel: (304) 284-0774
www.spinsterstreadle.com

US Felt Manufacturing Co.
61 Industrial Avenue
Sanford, ME 04073
Tel: (800) 444-3358
www.usfelt.com

The Woolery
PO Box 468
Murfreesboro, NC 27855
Tel: (800) 441-9665
www.woolery.com

Wooly Comforts
Box 2038
Chillicothe, OH 45601
Tel: (740) 775-1916
www.woolycomforts.com

The Yarn Source
2661 Highway 62 South, RR 1
Bloomfield, ONT K0K 1G0
Tel: (613) 393-2899
www.yarnsource.ca

Yarns

Handknitting.com
Laurel Murphy
1010 Brooklandwood Road
Lutherville, MD 21093-3701
www.handknitting.com

Herrschners
Customer Service
2800 Hoover Road
Stevens Point, WI 54481
Tel: (800) 441-0838
www.herrschners.com

Kertzer
6060 Burnside Court, Unit 2
Mississagua ON L5T 2T5
Canada
Tel: (905) 856-3447
www.kertzer.com

The Knitting Garden
75 County Road
North Falmouth, MA 02556
Tel: (888) 381-YARN
www.theknittinggarden.com

The Yarn Barn
5077 Andersonville Road
Dillwyn, VA 23936
Tel: (800) 850-6008
www.yarnbarn.com

Yarn Market
Yarnmarket, Inc.
12936 Stonecreek Drive, Unit D
Pickerington, OH 43147
Tel: (888) 996-9276
www.yarnmarket.com

Trimmings

BJ Craft Supplies
203 Bickford Road
Tivoli, TX 77990
www.bjcraftsupplies.com

Jo Ann Fabric and Crafts
www.joann.com

M&J Trimming
1008 Sixth Avenue
New York, NY 10018
Tel: (212) 204-9595
www.mjtrim.com

Michaels Arts and Crafts
www.michaels.com

Roxy Yarns
1131 McDonald Avenue
Brooklyn, NY 11230
www.roxyyarns.com

UMX, Inc.
21128 Commerce Point Drive
Walnut, CA 91798
Tel: (800) 755-6608
www.umei.com

Index

Acknowledgements

Thank you to everyone who helped with the book...

Julieta Brandào for supplying yarns and for making five of the bags (Alina, Scarlett, Annie, Harriet and Emma) and helping with the wet felting techniques.

Nicky Sanderson de la Peña and her mum, Marjorie, for providing me with Scottish sweaters for recycling.

Connie at Jamieson & Smith, Bev from knitting4fun, Jane Jubb at Sirdar, Twilleys of Stamford, Elle Yarns, DMC and Rowan for supplying yarns, and Lisa at U-Handbag for bag handles.

Amy, Alice and my daughter Lillie for modelling; and Paul Bricknell for the great photographs.

Last but not least, Corinne Masciocchi and Louise Coe for their help and support with planning and editing the book.